T0274646

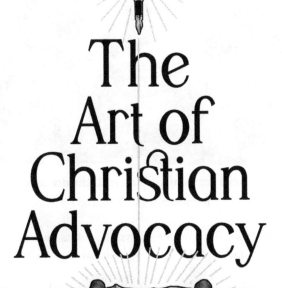

The
Art of
Christian
Advocacy

Christ seated disputing with the doctors
Rembrandt van Rijn, 1654

And so it was that after three days they found Him in the temple, sitting in the midst of the doctors, both hearing them and asking them questions.

And all who heard Him were astonished at His understanding and answers. Luke 2:46-47.

The Art of Christian Advocacy

JOHN WARWICK MONTGOMERY
Ph.D., D.Théol., LL.D.

& CRAIG A. PARTON
A.B., M.A., J.D.

ACADEMIC

Published by:
1517 Publishing
PO Box 54032
Irvine, CA 92619-4032

Publisher's Cataloging-In-Publication Data
(Prepared by The Donohue Group, Inc.)

Names: Montgomery, John Warwick, author. | Parton, Craig A., 1955– author. | Johnson, Philip, 1960– Historical bibliography of American legal apologetics.
Title: The Art of Christian Advocacy / John Warwick Montgomery, Ph.D., D. Théol., LL.D., and Craig A. Parton, Esq., J.D., M.A.
Description: Irvine, CA : 1517 Academic, [an imprint of New Reformation Publications], [2024] | "With Historical Bibliography of Legal Apologetics prepared by Philip Johnson." | Includes bibliographical references and index.
Identifiers: ISBN: 978-1-962654-81-4 (hardcover) | 978-1-962654-82-1 (paperback) | 978-1-962654-83-8 (ebook)
Subjects: LCSH: Apologetics. | Christianity and law. | Bible—Evidences, authority, etc. | Logic. | BISAC: RELIGION / Christian Theology / Apologetics. | PHILOSOPHY / Logic. | LAW / Legal Education.
Classification: LCC: BT1103 .M66 2024 | DDC: 239—dc23

Printed in the United States of America

Cover art by Zachariah James Stuef

CONTENTS

In Memoriam

Prof. Dr. Rod Rosenbladt
Christ College, Irvine

+

(d. February 2, 2024)

Dear Friend,

You have accepted a new and better citizenship,
where all recognize their need for an Advocate with
the Father, Jesus Christ the Righteous (1 John 2:1)

Veni Domine Iesu

PREFACE

In my first year of law school, a professor assured us, "Law school changes the way you think. Law school teaches disciplined thinking about matters you previously cared little for." He assured us we would notice it soon, perhaps over breakfast, when we realized we were reading the warranty on the toaster—and enjoying it.

Dr. John Warwick Montgomery and trial lawyer Craig Parton combined have spent two lifetimes thinking logically and rationally about the law and religious truth claims. Their experience is reflected in not only the *how* of advocacy but also the *why*. The *why* of every persuasive defender of the Christian religion is to get the person to face the key arguments for what C. S. Lewis called "Mere Christianity"—that is what the authors of this book do.

Using traditional logic, and also Biblical examples, the authors provide their readers with practical advice to make one a better thinker, advocate, and apologist, whether as a lawyer or layman.

Mark Lanier Esq.
Founder of Lanier Law and
the Lanier Theological Library

FOREWORD

The 1970s comedy show *Monty Python's Flying Circus* featured a skit where a man (Michael Palin) enters a clinic wanting to buy an argument. On his way to the room to argue, he mistakenly enters a room where he is loudly verbally assaulted by the occupant using the most vial names. It turns out he had entered the room for abuse, not argument! He eventually finds the correct room with John Cleese, and their exchange hilariously illustrates the bizarre nature of trying to commodify anything. Finally, Palin and Cleese argue about what an argument is: Cleese says that it can simply be the process of taking up a contrary position, while Palin insists that an argument is:

> A collection of statements, one of which is the argument's conclusion and the rest of which are the argument's premises, which are intended to support or justify the conclusion.

It is almost uncanny how this skit from over 50 years ago manages to typify much of modern public discourse. The condition of public debate is such that it is simply yelling at each other using terrible language and name-calling. This results in metaphorically hitting each other on the head with a hammer, another scene from the Monty Python skit. Palin had the right idea as to what an argument is, but he is missing the skill of advocacy.

Arguing for truth in today's public square or academic climate is challenging. Even *claiming* to *know* objective truth is a bold move and one that often results in the Monty

Pythonesque hitting with the hammer! However, the authors of the book you hold are courageous enough to assert absolute truth claims and provide the tools to properly advocate for such claims. The authors are saying that you *can* know for certain religious truth, and what's more, you should actually argue or advocate for that truth.

Both authors are lawyers, so it is not surprising that they revert to the skills arising from legal advocacy. The authors are aligned with a recent poll where over 90% of the members of the legal profession were of the view that oral argument has a very important impact on court hearings. This study revealed that maintaining oral advocacy in our justice system assists in access to justice, persuasion, and fairness and assists tribunals in deciding complex issues. The task of courts the world over is the same. According to the European Court of Human Rights, "all judicial conflict-resolution is to resolve by logic what would otherwise be resolved by arbitrariness, force, etc. The essence of the rule of law is that the logic of private force be replaced by the public force of logic." (*Nuutinen v. Finland*, No. 32842/96 ECHR, June 27, 2000). In other words, we need a rules-based justice system where evidence is admitted, and advocacy occurs before a neutral tribunal. That is what a functioning society based on the rule of law requires.

Modern advocacy has its roots in the 2500-year-old tradition of rhetoric. This ancient discipline is forensic-based and has as its focus the most effective and persuasive ways of organizing and focusing on an argument. Aristotle, Cicero, and others from the Greco-Roman world developed the rules and best practices of rhetoric to be used in court cases. Any modern textbook on legal advocacy pays tribute to this source and comments on the impact of classical thinking on today's great legal advocates.

Classical rhetoricians divided persuasive discourse into three categories: logical argument (*logos*), emotional argument (*pathos*), and ethical appeal or credibility (*ethos*). These divisions are not completely separate air-tight categories but are subject to overlap and connection. Aristotle, Cicero, and Quintillian wrote for laypeople who had to argue their own legal cases before judges who themselves were not necessarily trained professionals. This audience was the equivalent of today's self-represented, or *pro se*, litigants, who go to court to represent themselves. While today, we see the skills of advocacy as the exclusive domain of the legal profession, history has shown that it is simply an aspect of a good classical education.

Indeed, the importance of advocacy is best illustrated by the publication last year of a series of lectures given throughout the United Kingdom under the prestigious **Hamlyn Lectures** by Lord David Pannick K.C. In his book **Advocacy** (Cambridge University Press, 2023), Pannick cites classic sources of rhetoric, many historical examples, both good and bad, and his own experience as a barrister of more than 40 years. He concludes that advocacy is still so very important in deciding difficult issues. In fact, it holds a central place in the Anglo Common Law adversarial system:

> Oral argument is perhaps the most powerful force there is, in our legal process, to promote a change of mind by a judge. Judges in fact change their minds under the influence of oral argument and this is not an arcane feature of the system; it is at the centre of it. (**Advocacy** p. 152)

In applying the discipline of *advocacy* to Christian apologetics, the connections are plentiful, and the utility is obvious. Pannick's first principle of advocacy is to be prepared. As an advocate, one must be in command of all the relevant facts and the law. In the words of Cicero, an advocate cannot "be eloquent upon a subject that is unknown to him." This mastery seems to be what the Apostle Peter had in mind when encouraging a group of scattered and persecuted Christians throughout the Roman world to "always be prepared to make a defense (*apologia*) to anyone who asks you for a reason for the hope that is in you" (1 Peter 3:15).

Another helpful aspect from Pannick's list is how one "delivers" the message as an advocate. Similarly for an apologist—delivery with clarity and tone as to why one should accept Christianity's central message is all important. Pannick argues that the value of this important skill goes back to the times of Cicero and Quintillian. It is simply part of human nature to be more receptive as an audience to a presentation that is done in a respectful tone. Times may not have changed much since Cicero or even when Peter stated that one's "delivery" in giving a defense of the Gospel must be done "with gentleness and respect." It is almost as if the Apostle would have been aware of Cicero's injunction that "it is natural for judges to be more willing to believe those whom they find it easier to listen to."

Important principles of modern advocacy, as described by Lord Pannick, have many more parallels with Christian apologetics than the two stated above. Montgomery and Parton give the reader many of those principles. An important thing to remember is that these principles of advocacy are not reserved for lawyers or specialists in rhetoric. They are for everyone. Aristotle and Cicero wrote their material for laypersons. The art of persuasion or advocacy is for non-lawyers as well as lawyers. In his letter to the early Christians, Peter assumed his audience was composed of lay people—he did not write to the elders or deacons (what we would now call professional clergy). Just as evangelism is the task of the entire church, laity, and clergy alike, so is apologetics, according to the New Testament. A good apologist is a skillful advocate for the defense of the faith.

This is important because, in the everyday world, one need not be an "expert" to make determinations of truth and justice. Our system is built on the premise that a jury composed of lay people, properly instructed by a judge, can make decisions of life and death, legal responsibility, and monetary damages. Juries make decisions based on the evidence they have heard and the advocacy presented based on that evidence. That is the role of a juror, and that is the intended audience of the authors of this book.

The virtues of advocacy are applicable both inside and outside the courtroom. Competent and skillful advocacy is important not only in apologetics on this earth but also because all will face the final judgment before God in the next life, known as the *Great Assize*. This grand cosmic courtroom scene is described in the biblical material and in the Nicene Creed and is an event for which we should all be prepared. If all that good advocacy does is point out that we should not go unrepresented to that final courtroom scene, it will have served its purpose. Remember that the Apostle John—who was very concerned with witnesses, evidence, testimony, and truth—also warned his students that, as sinners, we all deserve God's judgment. He cautioned that going into the *Great Assize* unrepresented was foolish and that "we have an advocate with the Father, Jesus Christ the righteous" (1 John 2:1). The purpose of this book is to show that everyone needs the wholly sufficient and true "advocate" Jesus Christ to speak on our behalf at that critical moment.

Recently, the term "post-truth" became the "Word of the Year," and in joining our lexicon, it illustrates how objective facts are far less influential in shaping public opinion than appeals to emotion and personal belief. Our age is one where C. S. Lewis (in his work *The Abolition of Man*) predicted that "the head with its facts" would lose to "the belly with its emotions." As Lewis so eloquently stated throughout his writings, only the proclamation and defense of the Gospel found in God's revealed Word can respond to a culture absorbed with such devastating thinking. Montgomery and Parton, in this book, combat the "post-truth" of our era and articulate a way to defend and advocate the Gospel solution.

The Honourable Dallas K. Miller K.C.

A MODEST PREAMBLE

While the principles of persuasive advocacy set forth in this slender volume will benefit those of any profession or confession, it is uniquely designed for those who take seriously Saint Peter's admonition to "be ready always to give a **defense** (Gr. *apologia*) to those who ask, yet with gentleness and reverence." (1 Peter 3:15). Indeed the apostles were so adept at implementing this command that they "turned the world upside down" with their persuasive advocacy of the legally compelling evidence for Christian belief.

The purpose of this book is to explain that the art of advocacy and persuasion, when tied inextricably to the "many convincing proofs" (Acts 1:3) culminating in the factual resurrection of Jesus Christ, is deeply Biblical and is best seen as "logic **supplemented**" and not "logic **supplanted**." With good examples (and at other times, deplorable ones) from our profession, one will learn how to "think like a lawyer" when engaged in "giving a reason for the hope that is within" them.

Consider this work the culinary equivalent of an *amuse-bouche* (literally a "mouth teaser") that serves in fine restaurants as a mere introduction to a deeper feast we have endeavored to provide on an academic level for more than a quarter of a century at the Academy of Apologetics in Strasbourg, France (see www.apologeticsacademy.eu).

We remain under the all-sufficient imputed righteousness of Jesus Christ our Advocate . . .

Prof. Dr. John Warwick Montgomery

Craig A. Parton, J.D.
Feast of the Presentation of the Lord
February 2, 2024
Strasbourg, France

PART I
Lawyers and Legal Reasoning

We have all heard it said of someone: "He thinks like a lawyer." In spite of the generally negative public image of lawyers in our day, this characterization is usually a high compliment: It suggests clarity and precision of thought well above the average, coupled (perhaps) with a particular, arcane reasoning ability not shared by those outside the legal profession. In this book, we shall examine the reasoning process in general, together with those special styles of reasoning which lawyers and judges employ professionally. Our object (as is the case throughout this book) combines the "is" and the "ought": we wish to offer a clear description of legal reasoning and also provide some normative guidelines to assist in the improvement of your reasoning faculties.

PART I
Lawyers and
Legal Reasoning

Reason and the Law

Few disciplines have as intimate a concern with reasoning as the law. This is particularly clear from the concept of the "reasonable man" which serves as the underlying Common Law standard of judgment, particularly where foresight, care, and susceptibility to harm are concerned (*Vaughan v. Menlove*, [1837] 3 Bing. N.C. 468; *Heaven v. Pender*, [1883] 11 Q.B.D. 503). David Walker wryly observes in *The Oxford Companion to Law* that "Lord Bramwell occasionally attributed to the reasonable man the agility of an acrobat and the foresight of a Hebrew prophet, but the reasonable man has not the courage of Achilles, the wisdom of Ulysses, or the strength of Hercules, nor has he the prophetic vision of a clairvoyant." He is not a mystic; he uses his head. So all-pervasive is the reasonable man standard in the law that it has occasionally led to bizarre, anthropomorphic applications to the animal kingdom. The first example centers on the just-mentioned Baron Bramwell, and was highlighted by Mr. Justice Cardozo in the Yale Review, July, 1925: the second derives from an opinion of Rosenberry, C.J., in the American case of *Brown v. Travelers Indemnity Co.*, 251 Wis. 188, 193–194, 28 N.W. 2d 306 (1947).

Cardoza:

There is an opinion by Baron Bramwell which deals with the propensities of pigs. A fence was defective, and the pigs straying did mischief to a trolley car. The decision was that the barrier should have been sufficient to protect the adjoining owner against the incursions, not of all pigs, but of pigs of "average vigour and obstinacy." "Nor do we lay down," said the learned Baron, "that there must be a fence so close and strong that no pig could push through it, or so high that no horse or bullock could leap it. One could hardly tell the limits of such a requirement, for the strength of swine is such that they would break through almost any fence, if there were a sufficient inducement on the other side. But the company is bound to put up such a fence that a pig not of a peculiarly wandering disposition, nor under any excessive temptation, will not get through it." Perhaps the humor of this ruling was more unwitting than designed. Some may agree with Sir Frederick Pollock that the decision is "almost a caricature of the general idea of the 'reasonable man.'"

*   *   *

Chief Judge Rosenberry:

"Just what would happen after a cow on the highway is struck by an automobile is something that could not have been foreseen or anticipated by the plaintiff. What the cow did was the natural, reasonable and probable thing for her to do under the circumstance."

Setting aside reasonable pigs and cows, it would appear that Sir Edward Coke (d. 1634) was quite right when he declared in the Epilogue to his Commentary on Littleton that "reason is the soul of the law":

Ratio est anima legis: for then are we said to know the law, when we apprehend the reason of the law; that is, when we bring the reason of the law so to our owne reason, that as we perfectly understand it as our owne; and then, and never before, we have such an excellent and inseparable propertie and ownership therein, as we can neither lose it, nor any man take it from us, and will direct us (the learning of the law is so chained together) in many other cases. But if by your studie and industrie you make not the reason of the law your owne, it is not possible for you long to retaine it in your memorie.

But what exactly do we mean by "reason"?

The Reasoning Powers
Deductive Inference

To reason means to employ the inferential functions of the mind. Three principal kinds of inference are involved as one reasons: deduction, induction, and retroduction (or abduction). Unfortunately, these terms are often used very loosely, compounding confusion. Thus Dr. Watson often speaks of Sherlock Holmes' "deductive powers," when in fact Holmes generally engages in the process of induction!

As between deduction and induction, the "outstanding difference," observes G. W. Paton in his *Textbook of Jurisprudence*, "is the source of the major premise—the deductive method assumes it whereas the inductive sets out to discover it from particular instances." Deduction moves from the general to the particular, while induction starts with the particular to arrive at the general.

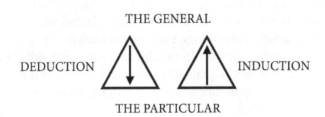

How is deduction employed in legal reasoning? A judge will reason from an accepted rule, or principle, or standard to a decision in a particular case. Setting aside the contemporary disagreements among such legal theorists as Hart, MacCormick, and Dworkin over the precise distinctions between rules, principles, and standards, we may illustrate as follows:

From the so-called "mailbox rule" in contract law (an offer or acceptance is effectively communicated when the offeror's or offeree's letter is posted, not when it is received, but the rescinding or rejection of an offer is effective only on receipt), a judge will deduce that A, whose acceptance of B's offer was mailed before B's letter rescinding the offer was received, can hold B to the contract.

From the principle of tort law that no one should be liable to pay damages in the absence of a showing of fault (cf. Dean Pound; 36 Harvard Law Review 641 [1923]), a judge may grant summary judgment against a plaintiff who has not been able to show that the defendant owed him any legal duty of care.

To be sure, as Dworkin has well argued in *Taking Rights Seriously*, principles are more general than rules. Rules have an all-or-nothing character about them, while principles often do no more than incline in a certain direction. Thus, one encounters torts of strict or absolute liability, where one maybe liable with no showing of negligence whatsoever— for example, in American or EC products liability law, or the *Rylands v. Fletcher*, [1868] L.R. 3, H.L. 330, scenario (followed as case law on both sides of the Atlantic) where one is held strictly liable for the escape from one's land of a non-natural entity likely to do mischief. In any event, whether the legal principle is qualified or unqualified, once that principle is made applicable to a particular case deductive inference is exhibited.

Standards are even more general than principles, as can be seen from the following example, again from the law of tort: Fault is present when one fails to behave as would an ordinary reasonable or prudent man (cf. Pound, *An Introduction to the Philosophy of Law* [1922]). We have already noted the maximal generality of the reasonable or prudent man standard in the Common Law: deductions in particular cases are continually made from the standpoint of such a hypothetical person (or pig? or cow?).

It is important to observe that, in the legal field at least, difficulties with deductive reasoning seldom have to do with the validity of the deduction as such. (Judges are generally strong on deductive logic—though we shall offer some sobering counter-examples shortly). The major difficulty in the deductive process focuses on the applicability of the rule/principle/standard to the particular facts of the case at hand; in other words, the dilemma is one of fact rather than logic. Consider the Irish case of *Gill v. McDowell*, [1903] 2 Ir. R. 463, in which the issue was whether the plaintiff, intending to buy 2 heifers and a bullock, or 2 bullocks and a heifer, could recover for breach of warranty or for deceit when in fact he was sold a bullock, a heifer, and a hermaphrodite! (Ruling: he could recover, based on a fairly questionable effort at bringing bovine sexual proclivities into line with general principles of express/implied warranty in the law of contract and the tort rules defining a prima facie case for deceit/fraud).

The Reasoning Process
Induction and Retroduction

Christie, in his *Jurisprudence*, has termed deductive analysis "relatively trivial"; that is doubtless an exaggeration, but surely inductive inference is far more central to the juridical reasoning process, at least in Common Law countries. Paton describes the inductive operation thusly: "Instead of starting with a general rule the judge must turn to the relevant cases, discover the general rule implicit in them." Dworkin (Law's Empire) has felicitously analogized this process to the writing of a chain novel:

> In this enterprise a group of novelists writes a novel seriatim; each novelist in the chain interprets the chapters he has been given in order to write a new chapter, which is then added to what the next novelist receives, and so on. Each has the job of writing his chapter so as to make the novel being constructed the best it can be, and the complexity of this task models the complexity of deciding a hard case under law as integrity.

Judges aim to move inductively from the facts of the particular case before them to a rule or principle that will best fit the stream of legal decision-making that has gone before. Each case is a new chapter in the continuing saga of the law and needs to carry it forward with maximum effectiveness.

Continental Civil Law systems historically stress deduction from codes (such the French Code Civil) to particular cases, but at the same time are unable to avoid inductive analysis from the cases (in French, *jurisprudence*). In contrast, Common Law systems such as our own have traditionally focused more on the inductive building up of the law through case decisions—though today entire areas of the Common Law are increasingly subject to statute (mini-codes), such as land law (the 1925 Property legislation, the Rent Acts) or the criminal law (the Theft Acts of 1968 and 1978) or Civil Procedure (the 1849 Field Code in California). While recognizing that Civil and Common Law necessarily contain both elements in variable proportions, we might characterize the classic difference diagrammatically:

Code systems	=	Case law systems
(Deduction)		(Induction)

But inductive inference, so fundamental to the scientific method, is not the straightforward, unidimensional process Francis Bacon thought it was (Bacon, not so incidentally, was both Lord Chancellor and the foremost theoretician of scientific method in the 17th century). There is an imaginative dimension to reasoning that transcends both deduction and induction. Charles Peirce, the 19th century philosopher, called it "abduction": today, it is generally referred to as "retroduction." Deduction, as it were, proves that something must be, since it is shown to follow from the premises or first principles of the system; induction demonstrates that something actually is operative, for one thereby discovers particular factual truths that lead to general conclusions; retroduction imaginatively endeavours to devise a theory that will best explain the facts. A striking illustration of the retroductive process from James Watson and Francis Crick, is the molecular structure of DNA (the nucleic acid bearing the blueprint of heredity):

Watson was convinced by reasons based upon genetics that [the] structure could only be built around two spirals arranged "in a certain way." The answer lay in this "certain way."

The only way of representing the three-dimensional structure of an invisible molecule is to replace atoms or groups of atoms by spheres and then build a model of the molecule.

This is exactly what Crick and Watson did, tirelessly attempting to arrange the two spirals. To quote the expression used by one of them, all of their models were "frightful," and quite inadequate to cope with DNA's known qualities ("You couldn't hang anything on these spirals") . . .

Then came the famous "spiral night." Crick was working late in a laboratory upstairs. On the ground floor, Watson also was going over a list of possible solutions. That night Crick had a revelation, a solution whispered to him by his intuition: there were only two spirals, they were symmetrical, and they coiled in opposite directions, one from "top to bottom" and the other from "bottom to top" (this hypothesis also reflected certain laws of crystallography).

Crick raced downstairs—it was a spiral staircase—and enthusiastically explained his theory to Watson. Watson received it calmly: it sounded simple to him, much too simple. Then, mentally, he built a spiral form based on this idea, and all the various chemical, biological and physical requirements he put forward were met by it. Now he too was excited; he paced up and down the laboratory, repeating: "It must be true, it must be true."[1]

Of course, the retroductive, imaginative solution still had to be tested inductively to establish its validity: but it was informed imagination, not the pedestrian application of deductive or inductive models, that led to this remarkable discovery.

---

1. Roger Louis, *Réalités*, September 1963.

A parallel illustration in law is Lord Atkin's Judgment in *Donoghue v. Stevenson*, [1932] A.C. 562. In that judgment, Lord Atkin revolutionized the English law of tort by setting forth the so-called "neighbour principle," a generalized definition of the duty of care applicable to all particular instances of negligence.

> The rule that you are to love your neighbour becomes in law, you must not injure your neighbour; and the lawyer's question, "Who is my neighbour?" receives a restricted reply. You must take reasonable care to avoid acts or omissions which you can reasonably foresee would be likely to injure your neighbour. Who, then, in law is my neighbour? The answer seems to be—persons who are so closely and directly affected by my act that I ought reasonably to have them in contemplation as being so affected when I am directing my mind to the acts or omissions which are called in question.

How did Atkin arrive at this remarkable principle? What the spiral staircase was to Watson and Crick, a Sunday church service was to Lord Atkin. Here is how Atkin's grandson described it, as quoted by Atkin's biographer Geoffrey Lewis:

> During the summer holidays of 1931, I was staying at Craig-y-don with other members of the family. In those days the family went to Matins at the Aberdovey Church every Sunday morning and there was a large family lunch with Aunts and cousins presided over by my Grandfather, who took much pride in his carving of the joint. He often used the carving time and the carving weapons to conduct a discussion. I remember on several occasions that the post-church discussion about the snail and the ginger beer bottle case—who is my neighbour?—was an easily understandable theme immediately after church.

Jesus' dialogue with a lawyer on the question, "Who is my neighbour?" encompassing the parable of the Good Samaritan (Luke 10:25–37), triggered Lord Atkin's thinking and led retroductively to the development of his neighbour principle.

Legal reasoning, like scientific method, focuses on "constructs" or "models." These are often arrived at through retroductive processes and are ultimately tested by their ability to "fit the facts"—the facts of the case at hand and the existing fabric of the chain novel of the law as it has been written, chapter by chapter, by judges who have gone before. Karl Popper, in his *Logic of Scientific Discovery*, uses analytical philosopher Ludwig Wittgenstein's analogy of the Net: "Theories are nets cast to catch what we call 'the world': to rationalize, to explain, and to master it. We endeavor to make the mesh ever finer and finer." Another analogy is that of the Shoe and the Foot: Our theories (here, legal reasonings) are like shoes, and the object is to fashion them so that they exactly fit the foot, i.e., the case at hand, set against the background of the developing legal tradition. We don't want a shoe like Procrustes' bed in Greek mythology: a bed of just one size into which all guests were fitted—by stretching them or even chopping them off on either end if they were very small or very big!

Too Many Logics?
Too Much Logic?

In an episode of the popular American television series, "The Paper Chase," based on a student's first year at Harvard Law School, a barber remarks that he had also been a law student for a short time: "Professor Kingsfield [the redoubtable contracts professor] told us that he was going to get rid of the mush in our heads. I decided that I *liked* the mush in my head."

Lawyers are sometimes criticized for the very fact that they are committed to rigorous, logical reasoning. This criticism can take two forms. First, it is said that the logic to which lawyers are committed is a narrow, "Western" style of reasoning, with no necessary application to the thought-forms of other cultures. Second, it is maintained (by some even within the legal professions themselves) that the law is too logical—too formalistic—insufficiently sensitive to social policy and change. What can be said to these criticisms?

The idea of the law shackled by "Western logic" can be dealt with fairly readily. **Logic properly has no plural**. That is to say, as historians of logic such as Kneale have shown, there is only one human reasoning faculty, not a multiplicity of logics. True, different cultures have used different symbol systems to represent logical argument, but the inferential processes (deduction, induction, retroduction) are always the same. To criticize logic as "Aristotelian" and therefore to reject it as "Western" because Aristotle, in the Western tra-dition, was the first to set out its principles in a formal way is the equivalent of rejecting plane geometry as "Western" because Euclid first formulated its proofs.

Inferential processes are inherent to the human being whatever his cultural milieu. Indeed, they must be pre-supposed in order to engage in any meaningful discus-sion or search for truth. Consider: any argument against logic already employs logic! And any collection of facts to disprove induction is already using inductive method! As Emerson said of Brahma: "When me they fly, I am the wings." So when a student friend doing a degree in poetry or Eastern religions tells you that he or she not bound by your Aristotelian, legalistic logic, just point out that that very argument is already dependent on the reliability of inferential reasoning.

But isn't the law too rational—too formalistic? Writes H. L. A. Hart, in his article on the philosophy of law in Paul Edwards' *Encyclopedia of Philosophy*: "What the critics intend to stigmatize by these terms is the failure of courts, when applying legal rules or precedents, to take advantage of the relative indeterminacy of the rules or precedents to give effect to social aims, policies, and values." Note that the criticism is not that lawyers are literally "too logical"; that would be as silly a criticism as "George is too honest," or "Nigel has too much integrity." The critic is actually saying that judges focus so much on conforming their decisions to the precedents—to writing the next chapter of the serial novel so it nicely fits the previous chapters—that they blind themselves to the real needs of the litigants and of the soci-ety of which they are part.

We shall discover that Hart's point here arises quite naturally from his belief, held by relatively few English legal scholars but by many American jurisprudents, that legal rules are "relatively indeterminate," that is, are largely ambiguous and able to be interpreted without great difficulty in support of very different and often contradictory legal conclusions. But even if we agreed with this viewpoint (which we do not) we should still do our utmost to oppose judgments based on Judges' personal perception of "social aims, policies, and values." Why? Because otherwise the distinction between judge and legislator becomes hopelessly blurred, and unelected judges declare the law as a mirror reflection of their own philosophies of life or beliefs as to which way the social winds are blowing. Precise legal reasoning ("formalism" if you will) is the only corrective to such an aberration, which is fully capable of destroying the essential separation of powers in a democratic society.

The late Professor Kales of the Northwestern University School of Law put it well in arguing for the strict exclusion of extrinsic evidence as to the nature of estates devised by will, since to allow such evidence is to open the door to subjective judicial determination and leave what should be rational decision-making to the whims of social policy (5 American Law and Procedure 141):

> It is believed that a great evil in the way wills are construed would be remedied, if Judges and courts would observe that, when the difficulty of construction has to do with the *state or character of the interest created*, outside evidence, of the state of the testator's family and other circumstances surrounding the making of the will, while legally admissible for what they are worth, are worth nothing except to induce a prejudice for one construction because it would be more likely to do justice between the parties, and to furnish the basis for wild speculation, without adequate proof, that the testator meant the words in the sense which to the court's mind would do this justice between the parties.

In sum, we suggest that larger considerations of justice and social policy ought properly to be introduced into the legal system by Parliament or Congress and discovered by judges in the fabric of the common law through the use of their best rational faculties—rather than be imposed by individual fiat from the bench. In the long term, solid legal reasoning would appear more capable of producing justice than ad hoc policy decisions which can, and so often do, unravel the law's existing fabric.

Logical Fallacies

If rationality is to be courted by the lawyer rather than given a limited scope of operation, what are the pitfalls he or she must guard against? In a word, fallacious reasoning must be identified and vigorously eschewed!

We shall now therefore identify some of the most common and egregious logical blunders, and illustrate them by way of one of the most atypical judges ever to have graced (we use the term loosely) an English bench: 19th century Serjeant Arabin, whose bizarre opinions have been collected by Vice-Chancellor Sir Robert Megarry (*Arabinesque-at-law*).

A. Material Fallacies

1) Faulty generalization (*jumping to a conclusion without sufficient evidence*).

   > *The Court* (Serjeant Arabin—hereinafter "SA"), *in charge*: This is a case from Uxbridge. I won't say a word, as can anyone doubt the prisoner's guilt?

   > Even if a number of criminals came from Uxbridge, it would not follow that **everyone** from Uxbridge was a criminal—or indeed that any given individual from that place were himself or herself a criminal!

2) Assuming the cause ("*post hoc, propter hoc*").

The medieval logicians illustrated this fallacy by the question: If two clocks strike the hour at the same moment, does that mean that one of them caused the other to strike? The answer, of course, is a resounding No. The mere fact that two things occur simultaneously or are related temporally in no way establishes a causal connection between them. Causation (as in tort actions) must be established independently.

3) Faulty analogy (*asserting something as analogous that is not*).

And when a prisoner stated that a policeman had refused to accompany him to the place where his employer was, the policeman was about to explain.

The Court (SA): Oh! you need not apologize. The police are not so polite as the Marquis of Hastings.

What had the Marquis of Hastings to do with the case? The analogy was not only absurd but indeed misleading. A proper analogy must be "on point" or should not be used at all.

4) False dilemma (*supposing that in a given situation there are only two alternatives when in fact there are more than two*).

The Court (SA) *in charge*: I cannot suggest a doubt: she goes into a shop, and looks at several things, and purchases nothing: that always indicates some guilt.

The Court offers only the alternatives of not going shopping or being found guilty of shoplifting! Surely, there is a third possibility?

5) Chronological Fallacy (*"argumentum ab annis"* or *the age of an idea tells you its value*).

    This is the effort to destroy an idea by dating it, e.g., "There they go again trying to impose their Victorian prudishness on everybody else!" Conversely, we mean to give prestige to an idea when we say it is "scientific" or "progressive" or "has been accepted since at least the Enlightenment."

    In short, if you can show that the idea came from the "Dark Ages" or is "positively Medieval," you need say nothing more about it.

6) Word magic (*using sophisticated grammar in an illogical manner to hide or obscure an obvious, and usually not very flattering, truth*).

    We are a culture of euphemisms: garbage collectors are now "sanitation engineers," a tax increase is now a "revenue enhancement," and "she died" is now "she passed away."

    Illustrative of this use of fantasy language to mask a simply stated and blunt truth, is the story told of the Old Wild West times. A man wanted to notify the family of the death of a member of that family who ran afoul of the law and had been hanged. After weeks of struggling to break the news, he wrote the family as follows: "It is with deep regret that I have to inform you that your son died recently while taking part in a public ceremony. The platform on which he was standing gave way."

B. Psychological Fallacies

1) Emotive language.

    The Court (SA), *in charge*: Can you suppose that this is a fabricated story founded on falsehood, with no foundation in truth, because she swears—that is, that her credit is not good, because she marked these sovereigns to entrap—that is, you see, the property is found upon her, and she has it?

"Fabricated story founded on falsehood": emotionally charged expressions (here aided and abetted by alliteration!) can go far to obscure the truth. Demagogues—and unscrupulous advocates—use this technique frequently.

2) Appeal to authority ("*but 'X' also believes it to be true as I do and 'X' is a Nobel Prize winner*").

The Court (SA): Ah, I knew I was right. I was quite sure your face was well known to me.

Such assertions were merely part of the Court's proclaimed omnicompetent infallibility:

'I know what's what';
'I never forget anything';
'I am not a fool'; and
'We have not lived here all our lives
for nothing.'

Serjeant Arabin here presents himself as the Grand Pooh-Bah, but this fallacy even more often consists of citing sane other sources as authority—without bothering to show the soundness of that alleged authority's arguments. Mere citation of an authority proves nothing. In courts of law, expert witnesses must be demonstrably qualified, or at least stipulated to as experts by both parties, in order for them to testify. And their testimony is subject to rigorous cross-examination.

3) Impressing by large numbers ("But the 300 who signed the *statement each hold a Ph.D.—they can't **all** be wrong*").

   Some years ago, a book was published with the title: *How To Lie With Statistics*. In point of fact, fifty million Frenchmen can be wrong. In the Middle Ages, virtually everyone believed that the sun went around the earth; this did not make it so.

4) Damning by origin ("*consider the source*").

   The inhabitants of Uxbridge not only were criminal but also attained the ultimate in *dexterity*:

   > *The Court* (SA): I assure you, gentlemen, they will steal the very teeth out of your mouth as you walk through the streets. l know it from experience.

   The source or origin of something is never sufficient to establish its value. Thus, ammonia is said to have been discovered by the alchemist Brandt while he was boiling toads in urine; the value of ammonia may safely be said to transcend the circumstances of its discovery!

5) Ad hominem ("*to the man*").

   > *The Court* (SA), *in charge*: He was a brickmaker. Now, we all know what a brickmaker's character is—at least l do.

   "*Ad hominem*" means arguing with reference to personalities ("to the man") rather than—properly—in reference to the point at issue ("*ad argumentum*"). At election time, it is common practice to denigrate one's opponent rather than face the issues he or she raises.

6)   Apriorism ("*invincible ignorance*").

Apriorism (from the Latin *a priori*—to reason from an unproven first premise) occurs when one assumes facts not in evidence, or when one presents as self-evident, eternal truth what in fact needs to be demonstrated. This is illustrated by the *a priori* held by the Englishman that England had never lost a battle. When given overwhelming evidence of such a clear defeat at battle, his response was always "Why now you don't consider ***that*** to be a battle, do you?"

C. Formal Fallacies

1)   The undistributed middle.

> *The Court* (SA), *in charge*: The business of this great metropolis must be carried on, and tradesmen must be protected in the exercise of their functions; so it will be for you to say whether the prisoner is guilty.

A proper syllogistic argument has the form:

Major Premise:	If A, then **B**	All dogs have fleas
Minor Premise:	If **B**, then C	Fleas cause suffering
Conclusion:	If A, then C	All dogs suffer

An illogical argument with an "undistributed middle" has the form:

Major Premise:	If A, then **B**	All elephants have big ears
Minor Premise:	If C, then **B**	Socrates has big ears
Conclusion:	If A, then C	Socrates is an elephant

Note that here the middle term ("B") is undistributed, i.e., functions in the same capacity in both the major and the minor premises, in contrast with its distributed functioning in the valid argument preceding. Such illogicality of form is exceedingly common.

2) Circularity and question-begging (*"petitio principii"*).

> *The Court* (SA), *in charge*: Law is founded on common sense, and those who take it for their guide in matters of fact and plain sense, will generally come to an ultimate conclusion; and all property depends upon particular circumstances. If this had not been marked, there would not have been a mark upon it.

A circular argument presupposes its own conclusion, that is, the conclusion is already contained in its assumptions. The result, of course, is no proof at all, but simply a restatement of the premises in another form. Such an argument is like many religious people who claim their particular holy book is divinely inspired because it *says* it is divinely inspired! As Rodgers and Hammerstein put it in The Sound of Music: "Nothing comes from nothing."

D. Unverifiability ("This isn't right; it isn't even wrong").

> *The Court*, to witness: Did you ever buy a horse of the prisoner?
>> Witness: No.
>> The Court: Then you did not pay him a five-pound note for that horse?
>> Payne, for prisoner: I am about to submit—
>> The Court: I cannot hear you. I know what you are about to say; and it is so monstrous and preposterous.

Here the court allows for no verifiability—or indeed falsifiability. But some arguments by their very nature permit no confirmation or disconfirmation. For example: Ghosts exist, but never show themselves when a competent investigator is present. As the physicist Wolfgang Pauli wrote in the margin of a colleague's scientific paper: "This isn't right; it isn't even wrong." Assertions unverifiable in principle are analytically meaningless-as well as being a colossal waste of court time.

The Peculiarities
of Legal Reasoning

In the most fundamental sense, "thinking like a lawyer" means simply "thinking clearly and logically." Logic has no plural, and there is no special "logic" for members of the legal professions. The presence of a fair amount of "mush" in the heads of most people causes the lawyer to stand out who properly uses his inferential capacities. The rigorous demands of legal argument generally separate the logical sheep from the irrational goats [*pace* Serjeant Arabin].

But clearly there are special twists to legal reasoning—unique characteristics that set it apart from the thinking employed by the man on the Clapham omnibus. Though these do not constitute a different logic or a unique type of inference, they require our close attention, for they will provide us with a valuable entrée into the law's domain.

1) Analogy.

False analogy, as we have seen, is a common type of logical fallacy. But proper analogy is the lawyer's strong suit. As early as the 13th century, Henry de Bracton wrote, at the outset of his treatise *De legibus*:

Should there emerge any new and un-wonted cases, or cases which have never before been dealt with in the realm, if there have been cases of similar nature, they should be decided by analogy (*per simile*), for it is a good occasion to proceed from like to like.

Illustrations of analogy reasoning in the law are legion. In an American case, the great Justice Oliver Wendell Holmes, Jr., argued (*Merchants' National Bank v. Wehrmann*, 202 U.S. 295, 26 S.Ct. 613 [1906]):

> It recently has been decided that a national bank cannot take stock in a new speculative corporation, with the common double liability in satisfaction of a debt. A fortiori, it cannot take stock in a partnership to the same end.

2) Distinction.

> *Denny v. Radar Industries, Inc.*
>   Court of Appeals of Michigan
>   28 Mich. App. 294; 184 N.W.2d 289 (1970)
>   John H. Gillis, Judge.
>
> "The appellant has attempted to distinguish the factual situation in this case from that in *Renfroe v. Higgins Rack Coating and Manufacturing Co., Inc.* (1969), 17 Mich. App. 259, 169 N.W.2d 326. He didn't. We couldn't. Affirmed. Costs to appellee."

If one's opponent offers as precedent an analogous past decision which appears to be "on all fours" with the instant case, what do you do? You attempt to show that the analogy does not hold at the crux of the issue: you distinguish that case from the present one, arguing that even if the court was correct in reaching the earlier decision, now it needs to come to a different result.

Note how Lord Herschell, in *Davis v. Shepstone*, L.R.11 A.C. 187, 190, distinguished criticism of the official acts of a public figure—not defamatory, because protected by qualified privilege and the right to fair comment—from the slanderous claim that the plaintiff had engaged in specific acts.

It is one thing to comment upon or criticise, even with severity, the acknowledged or proved acts of a public man, and quite another to assert that he has been guilty of particular acts of misconduct illegalities.

3) Legal Fictions ("As if" Reasoning).

Lawyers and judges frequently employ "as if" argumentation to bring new and unexpected fact situations within the ambit of existing case law and statute. In 37 Yale Law Journal 299 (1928), the following striking example is given:

> A Brooklyn traffic court last summer decided that a hearse is a pleasure vehicle. The issue was whether hearses should drive in a traffic lane assigned to pleasure vehicles or in another traffic lane assigned to trucks and other commercial vehicles. The propriety of the decision, I take it, is unquestioned.

A particularly all-embracing use of the legal fiction is the concept of "legal personhood." At law, a corporation is treated in many respects as if it were a human person. The caution with which such "as if" reasoning must be treated is illustrated by the slave cases, in which, prior to the abolition of slavery, biological persons were refused full legal personhood, as were Jews during the Third Reich and (some would say) unborn children under many supposedly civilized legal systems today.

4) "Would Be" Reasoning.

Legal logic frequently employs *reductio ad absurdum*: taking something to its logical—and negative—conclusion, and on this ground rejecting it. Said the great Lord Coke: "An argument based upon the would-be undesirable consequences of a contrary rule or decision is of the greatest weight in law" (Co. Litt. 66a, 97b).

An illustration is provided by the leading case of *Rylands v. Fletcher*, referred to earlier in this book. Why did the Court arrive at the rule that liability without proof of fault attaches to the consequences of the escape of a dangerous instrumentality from one's land? In part because otherwise—if it were necessary for the plaintiff to prove negligence in all such cases (for example, in the defendant's handling of his boa constrictors or dynamite)—defendants would often cause appalling harm and get away with it, owing to the propensities of the instrumentalities to produce great damage even when all due precautions have been taken. Strict liability is justifiable because a lesser level of liability would yield a *reductio ad absurdum*—or at least a *reductio ad detrimentum*.

5) Probability Reasoning.

The law operates on the basis of probabilities, not possibilities or absolute certainties. In a civil case, the Common Law standard of proof is the preponderance of evidence: on balance, the side with the greater weight of evidence (even 51%) wins. The criminal standard is much higher, for the stakes are correspondingly higher: a guilty verdict may be arrived at only if the triers of fact are convinced of guilt "to a moral certainty, beyond reasonable doubt." Note: not absolute certainty, or beyond **all** doubt—since (as the analytical philosophers have emphasized) no matter of fact can be demonstrated absolutely—but to a very high standard of probability.

Laymen have particular difficulty appreciating such probability reasoning, for in daily life we often operate on mere possibilities—and generally to our loss. ("We just may love each other—off to The Elvis Chapel in Vegas we go"). The law's standards are higher, as well they might be, considering the gravity of the issues with which it deals.

Similarly, laymen are often hard put to understand the strict rules of evidence applied by the criminal courts in England (and by both criminal and civil courts in the United States). Why, for example, should logically relevant and otherwise credible testimony be excluded simply because it comes from second-hand sources? Why should past convictions be kept from the jury, when they surely tell us a great deal about the accused? The answer is that where juries function as the trier of fact (as they do in the more serious criminal cases in England and also in most civil cases in America by Constitutional warrant) the law is scrupulous to ensure that they not be misled. Hearsay testimony is not subject to cross-examination, so its weaknesses might never be apparent to the jury. Knowledge of past convictions might result in a conviction based an already punished past crimes rather than on genuine evidence that the accused committed the crime for which he is now on trial.

In short, even when legal reasoning appears bizarre to the uninitiated, it generally (though, of course, not always, by virtue of human fallibility) reflects that *ratio* or reasonableness which Lord Coke saw as the soul of the law.

Rationality and Rhetoric

If the soul of the law is reason, why does so much of legal activity focus on advocacy, persuasion, and rhetoric? If facts and logic are determinative, why is advocacy needed at all? Doesn't advocacy function like the ancient Greek sophists who, according to Socrates, "made the worst argument appear the better"?

One response is the well-known aphorism of Oliver Wendell Holmes, Jr.: "The life of the law is not logic but experience." Holmes rightly emphasises that there is more to the law than rationality: but what he calls "experience" needs further specification.

As we have seen, legal systems exist primarily as dispute-resolution devices, resolving those intractable conflicts in a society that would otherwise rend the social fabric. The law thus almost invariably focuses on disputes—in which each side seeks to persuade an independent trier of fact of the correctness of its position. In such an adversarial context (and even the continental Civil Law's inquisitorial approach is but another style of resolving differences between adversaries), the field is not solely occupied by reason.

Logic, as applied to case law and statute and to the facts of the instant case, will need to be presented so persuasively that the trier of fact will accept that interpretation rather than the opponent's viewpoint. Inevitably, therefore, the presentation of the case will be of crucial importance. Logic will be supplemented by semantics and rhetoric—the choice of words and the style of presentation—the ultimate object being effective advocacy. Note well: logic supplemented, not supplanted. To present one's solidly-founded case with the best skills of advocacy is not to denigrate reason, but to make it the more effective.

In this respect, the law is no different from life in general (Holmes's "experience"). A logical argument, no matter how powerful, does not necessarily win the day.

Suppose you want to persuade the girl of your dreams to marry you. Is it enough to give her a carefully prepared, logical argument—based on impeccable deductive, inductive, and retroductive inference—proving that her characteristics and yours are ideally compatible? Important as those arguments are, your presentation—your advocacy, if you will—as represented by moonlight, flowers, and expressions of love, will be vital in obtaining a favorable verdict!

But have we not opened the door to the common stereotype of the unscrupulous and manipulative lawyer? Can advocacy not be employed to obscure the truth rather than make it persuasive? The answer, of course, is that skills of advocacy can be misused as well as properly employed—just as a hammer can be used not only to build a house but also to smash in the neighbor's skull. The value of a tool is not determined by its possible misuse. What our analysis should remind us of is the great potential harm that can be done by unethical lawyers, and the immense need for persons with a solid value system to enter the legal professions. Too much is at stake in a complex modern society for the legal system to be peopled other than by individuals with the highest standards of integrity.

Improving Your Rational Faculties

If, at the outset of this book, you suspect that your head is not entirely free of "mush," what can you do about it? Here are some suggestions:

1. Read and study a good book on logic, scientific method, and semantics. One of the best is *Critical Thinking* by Cornell University professor Max Black, one of the great interpreters of Wittgenstein. Black's book contains useful self-testing exercises.

2. Take a university, college, or further education course in logic. Warning: stick to classic ("Aristotelian") logic, hopefully combined with scientific method and semantics; courses in "modern logic," i.e., symbolic or existential logic, are too rarified and esoteric to be helpful to the student or legal practitioner.

3. Practice reading a daily news source and journal articles with a view to discovering fallacies of reasoning. Keep a file of illogicalities.

4. Engage in structured debate (for example, in the context of a debating society or club) as often as you can. You will thus be forced to analyze an opponent's arguments and improve on them.

5. Finally (by now you surely saw this coming) consider pursuing the law as a profession. The discipline of

reading and critiquing cases will in itself sharpen your reasoning faculties in ways that will surprise even you. The cases will put you in contact with some of the finest minds in history (and some not so fine). The best is likely to rub off on you, if you give it the opportunity. Like it or not, the United States at least is a reflection of critical Supreme Court cases like *Marbury v. Madison*, *Dred Scott*, *Brown v. Board of Education*, *Miranda v. Arizona*, *Roe v. Wade*, and *Dobbs v. Jackson Women's Health Organization*.

Suggested Readings

Burton, Steven J. *An Introduction to Law and Legal Reasoning.* Boston: Little, Brown, 1985.

Holland, James A. and Webb, Julian S. *Learning Legal Rules.* London: Blackstone, 1991.

Hubien, Hubert (ed.). *Le raisonnement juridique, Legal Reasoning. Die juridische Argumentation*, Proceedings of the World Congress for Legal and Social Philosophy, 1971. Brussels: Emile Bruylant, 1971. Essays in English, French, and German.

Jensen, O. C. *The Nature of Legal Argument.* Oxford: Blackwell, 1957.

MacCormick, Neil. *Legal Reasoning and Legal Theory.* Oxford: Clarendon Press, 1978.

Schlag, Pierre and Skover, David. *Tactics of Legal Reasoning.* Durham, N.C.: Carolina Academic Press, 1986.

Twining, William and Miers, David. *How to Do Things with Rules.* London: Weidenfeld and Nicolson, 1976.

Zelennyer, William. *The Process of Legal Reasoning.* Englewood Cliffs, N.J.: Prentice-Hall, 1963.

PART II
The Lawyer as Advocate

Introduction

Lawyers and legal reasoning were the subjects of Part 1 of this treatise—the emphasis was necessarily on logic and methods of reasoning, and on the purpose and function of the law, and how lawyers are professionally trained to deal with questions of fact based on sophisticated and long-settled rules of evidence.

While we began by looking at what the purpose and function of the legal system is and the central role that *evidence* plays in that system, we now want to examine the role of the lawyer as *advocate* and the art of persuasion. More specifically we want to take those principles of persuasion as developed by trial lawyers and see how they might apply to presenting the Christian position to skeptics in our age.

In Part I we made the assertion that advocacy is "logic **supplemented**" and **not** "logic **supplanted**." Part 2 endeavors to establish precisely that assertion.

But first, a word about Lawyers and Religion . . .

Lawyers, Religion and Christianity

A Toxic Trinity?

The authors between them have practiced as trial lawyers for over six decades, with one being the former Chairman of the Litigation Section of the Bar Association and Managing Partner of a 25-member law firm and Chairman of its highly regarded Litigation Department. We, therefore, can say with considerable experience that lawyers are not exactly "naturally religious" nor prone to emotional appeals to "just have faith." Why then is there a long history of lawyers being attracted to investigating the claims of Christianity in particular?

It is actually not surprising that a religion based on factual claims, that welcomes having its evidences checked out, and that challenges the serious inquirer to critically examine the evidence for the fundamental claim that Jesus Christ rose from the dead in verifiable history, would draw the attention of the legally trained. From the Apostle Paul in the 1st century, to Tertullian of Carthage in the 3rd century; to Jean Calvin at the time of the Reformation, to Hugo Grotius (the so-called "Father of International Law" in the 16th century and author of the first textbook on "apologetics" or the defense of the Christian position), to Sir Matthew Hale (Lord High Chancellor under Charles II in the 17th century), to William Blackstone

(codifier of the English common law in the 18th century),
to Simon Greenleaf (Professor of Evidence at the Harvard
Law School in the 19th century and author of the defini-
tive 3-volume work of its time modestly entitled, simply,
"*Greenleaf on Evidence*"), to Lord Hailsham (former Lord
High Chancellor in the 20th century), to John Warwick
Montgomery today, the list of the legally-trained who have
applied their advocacy skills to presenting Christian truth
claims is simply staggering.[1]

Not only have lawyers contributed to the defense of
the central claims of the Christian faith, but they have also
developed sophisticated rules or principles of advocacy or
persuasion, refined within the bubbling cauldron of the
common law adversarial system, and its progeny the jury
trial, to maximize receptivity to those claims. Those principles of advocacy or persuasion are what we will, in a
moment, turn our attention to. But first . . .

What is it about Christianity that trial lawyers have
found so uniquely attractive over the ages? Fundamentally,
Christianity is based on certain facts being true—refute these
facts and the religion crumbles *by its own admission* (see esp.
1 Corinthians 15:14 in the New Testament). Christianity
turns out to be not only verifiable but falsifiable (produce
the body of Christ and the entire religion is a fraud and its
claims can be summarily dismissed and a directed verdict
entered in favor of the skeptic). Therefore, Christianity is
inextricably tied to the world of fact and evidence, which

---

1. See articles on Simon Greenleaf and John Warwick Montgomery
in *History of Apologetics: A Biographical and Methodological
Introduction*. Forrest, Chatraw, McGrath eds. (Grand Rapids:
Zondervan, 2020); see Ross Clifford, *Leading Lawyers' Case for the
Resurrection* (Edmonton: Canadian Institute for Law, Theology and
Public Policy, 1996); and see also Philip Johnson's exhaustive bibliog-
raphy of legal apologists, which is Appendix C to this work.

is necessarily the domain of the legal system and lawyers by profession.

Simply put, Christianity is the only "faith founded upon fact"[2] and those facts can be established in precisely the same way **any** facts of history are established.

---

2. See the classic work by this title, namely Montgomery, *Faith Founded on Fact: Essays in Evidential Apologetics* (Irvine: New Reformation Press, 2015).

Effective Advocacy as the *Sauce Béarnaise* on the Filet de Boeuf of the Gospel

That said about the centrality of the factual **content** of Christian proclamation, it is still the case that the winsome **presentation** of that faith founded on fact requires the application of the *art* of persuasion as a fundamental piece of Christian proclamation.

Consider this analogy: While one critical aspect of a restaurant possessing a highly coveted Michelin star is the quality of the ingredients used, the artistry of the presentation of the cuisine is equally critical. The dishes must appeal to all aspects of the senses including sight and not just taste (both the aesthetic presentation of the meal as well as its taste are "rated" along with the demeanor, competency and professionalism of the full range of attending staff).

What we are suggesting is that legal advocacy principles are like the *Sauce Béarnaise* on a perfectly grilled filet de boeuf, or the garlic and butter sauce that forms a kind of burbling hot tub for the humble yet stately escargot. Or consider the careful application of the principles of oral advocacy, as practiced by trained advocates in the law, as the perfect crystal stemware in which resides a 1954 Chateau Lafite Rothschild. To be sure, one can guzzle such a wonder in a mere Styrofoam cup if so desired and the substance or contents remain a 1954 Chateau Lafite Rothschild—but

Riedel Bordeaux stemware is the perfect complimentary vessel or form in which to deliver such an exceptional wine.

Similarly, the advocate of the Gospel can (like a great sauce or exquisite stemware) enhance the receptivity of his audience to the message or (like a plain and plebeian plastic cup) be an utter hindrance to that reception.

The Advocate and
the Rhetorical Triangle

Classical principles of oral persuasion or rhetoric are sometimes referred to as the "rhetorical triangle," which encompass the concepts of content, empathy, and ethical appeal, or *logos*, *pathos* and *ethos*. Each angle of this triangle has a unique communicative function.

Logos asks: Does the advocate have real substance or **content** that is worth giving attention to?

Pathos asks: Does the advocate **care** about the listener and their condition or are they hellbent on only winning an argument, or making the sale, or having the last word? This is the emotive quality of the advocate and it is critical to the audience not concluding it is being manipulated or marketed.

Ethos asks: Are the advocate's basic life commitments consistent with what they say and teach? This is the issue of the *credibility* of the advocate. Unfortunately, it is not difficult to find negative illustrations of this principle. Most recently the internationally renowned Christian apologist and speaker Ravi Zacharias was found to have a complete double life of sexual immorality. His ethos scorecard showed a flat 0 and as English barrister Leslie Cuthbert puts it: "Credibility is very much like virginity. Once you lose it, it's impossible to regain."[3]

---

3. Leslie Cuthbert, 365 *Daily Advocacy Tips* (Great Britain: Bloomsbury Publ., 2015), at p. 356.

The most effective advocates are solid in all 3 areas—but extraordinary strength in one arm of the triangle can often be misused to "mask" weakness in another arm. In Christian proclamation, in particular, the temptation is to cover up how thin the *logos* or content piece is that is being presented (which should be centered on the facticity of the resurrection and the concomitant use of the legal-historical method to present the Gospel, a method described below) by displaying overwhelming *pathos* or empathy for the condition of the audience, or even focusing solely on *ethos* by substituting the advocate's subjective personal testimony at the expense of the *extra nos* objectivity of the *logos* of the Gospel (one thinks of the Baptist hymn: "He touched me and I am no longer the same"). Most religions have "He-She-It touched me" conversion stories (see William James, *Varieties of Religious Experience*) and this cannot be the arbitrator of truth claims. Both Mormons and Scientologists have been "touched and are no longer the same."[4]

If one must err on emphasizing one particular arm of the triangle, it certainly should be the *logos* side. Get the content of the central message clear and straight and primary.

Pathos is a natural by-product of a Gospel message that is presented as being for "sinners"—a designation that applies directly to the advocate also and even at the advocate's most victorious moment! The advocate should be very wary of announcing in public the positive results of his supposed changed life.

---

4. James' volume looks at cross-cultural religious experience and the universality of the "conversion testimony" in all religions. After researching mystic conversions in Buddhism, Christianity, Sufism and indeed the "whole field of religion," James concludes that "primarily religion is a biological reaction." William James, *Varieties of Religious Experience* (London: Longmans, Green & Co., 1907), at pp. 379–429, 504.

The renowned Christian philosopher and apologist Frances Schaeffer had *pathos* in abundance—it made him even feel terribly sorry for Bishop Pike when they debated. The result? There was no clear winner in the eyes of neutral observers of the debate! Jerry Falwell thought he had an impressive stockpile of *ethos* as head of the Moral Majority—but he was actually perceived as hardly that.[5] Mother Teresa oozed ethos though she seemed totally unaware of her power in that regard. Ethos is like that: those that think they have it, generally don't.

---

5. Jimmy Swaggert, the disgraced tele-evangelist, appalled not a few attendees at his 1986 debate with Muslim evangelist Ahmed Deedat in Baton Rouge, Louisiana when he noted in his opening statement (which has been transcribed) that he knew next to nothing about the Koran and was not a Bible scholar, and that he deeply regretted making past derogatory remarks about the Koran. He then invited the audience to pray with him.

The Advocate in the New Testament

We must first answer the question: Does the New Testament put a value on thoughtful and skilled *advocacy*?

Persuasive advocacy in the New Testament is looked upon very favorably. Illustrations abound of the "art of persuasion" being gainfully employed by the original Apostles as they "reasoned daily in the marketplace with whoever was present" (which was predominately Greek philosophers) and often in the synagogue (with Jewish teachers) "as was their habit." The synagogue in particular offered the common ground of the Old Testament and was the obvious starting block for proving Jesus was the Messiah prophesized of in the Old Testament. (See Paul in Athens in Acts 17:2–4, 16–34). Note that the advocacy took place in the "marketplace" or the home turf of the Athenians. Common ground with the Athenians was the result of Paul "observing closely" i.e., studying (Acts 17:16–17) their idols or false belief systems. Compare this approach with that of many Christians today who will not study cultural and other objections to Christianity for fear of being infected.

For example, the Egyptian Jew Apollos is described very favorably as "an eloquent man and mighty in the Scriptures" and able to "vigorously refute . . . publicly" those who opposed him, and the *logos* of his presentation was proving from the Scriptures that Jesus was the Messiah foretold in the Old Testament. (Acts 18:24–28).

Paul, a lawyer trained "at the feet" of Gamaliel a renowned Jewish Supreme Court Judge (Sanhedrin) in Palestine (Acts 22:3), is an example of the full inculcation of the rhetorical triangle: his *logos* is always the historical Christ "who suffered under Pontius Pilate" and the resurrection presented as analytic "verification" explicitly confirmed by miracle and prophecy and contemporaneous eye-witness accounts. But Paul had *pathos* for his audience (rather himself be accursed than see his Jewish brethren lost—Romans 9:3), and *ethos* (refused to live off others—made tents) so that he ("and those with him") would not be an economic burden to his hosts—Acts 20:34–35; reminds his audience at Ephesus that he did not neglect to give them the "whole counsel of God." (Acts 20:27). Paul had *ethos* in a life lived consistently in line with his beliefs.

Principles of Persuasion from the Law as Applied to the Legal Defense of the Biblical Gospel

The Advocate and the Audience

> **Advocacy Principle No. 1**: An effective advocate understands and considers the views of the audience and the particular existing cultural climate, but never at the expense of diluting or compromising the content of the message.

In discussion with skeptics this means that the presentation of the Gospel recognizes unique objections that a particular culture poses but never compromises the critical elements of that changeless message to accommodate the latest philosophical, moral or ethical fashions. Indeed, our message is exceedingly timely because it is utterly timeless. "Jesus Christ the same yesterday, today and forever." (Hebrews 13:8).

> **Advocacy Principle No. 2**: An effective advocate will, through rigorous and diligent study and exhaustive preparation, find at least *initial common ground* with their audience.

The effective advocate communicates that they in some sense walk in similar shoes as their audience. For example, there is at least *one* common ground even between cannibals and normal members of the human species in that both can be said to enjoy eating—one enjoys leg of lamb (*gigot d'agneau*), while the other is a connoisseur of *gigot d'homo-sapiens*. Cuisine, thus, becomes a common point of shared humanity from which a deeper conversation can take place.

The most effective advocates are serious students of their audience and (if the context is a debate) their opponent, and will study and prepare so that they understand the prevailing Zeitgeist of their audience. In short, effective advocates are also *careful and observant listeners* in order to discern points of resistance in their audience to considering the Gospel.

Barrister Cuthbert puts it nicely: "Another error advocates regularly make is to simply listen for points with which they can disagree." (Cuthbert, *supra* at ft. 3, p. 58).

Paul at Athens is the textbook example of an observant and careful listener—he had walked around cultural Athens and "observed" their theology. The result? Paul concluded that the citizens of Athens had an altar to a god for every occasion and even an altar to "the unknown god" just in case they missed one. Paul starts with common ground with the Athenians in a Creator God and citations to their own poets Aratus (271–213 B.C.) and Cleanthes (330–230 B.C.), but does not stop there. It hits the proverbial fan when Paul speaks of Christ being "risen from the dead." (Acts 17:22–34[6]).

The effective Christian advocate asks: What unique cultural factors (good and bad) have been consciously or unconsciously imbibed by the audience and culture you seek to penetrate with the Gospel? One must be aware of the particular hurdles to the Gospel in other cultures. Presenting the Gospel in the Baptist District of Alabama is assuredly different than presenting the Gospel in the Castro District of San

---

6. This raises an interesting issue: What if talk of rising from the dead or a resurrection is totally offensive to your audience? Compromise on that and the Gospel can in no sense be considered to have been presented.

Francisco. To not get this spells the doom of the Christian advocate who may never see his lack of diligent study and preparation as the true cause of his lack of impact.

Study to be prepared for current objections to Christianity that were not even contemplated in the past 2000 years of Christian history and which the apologist must be ready to address—e.g., the current cultural orthodoxy that "one chooses one's sexual identity and this can be a constantly dynamic and evolving process," or that "the God of the Bible really especially and uniquely hates homosexuals," or that "evidence means very little when in the final analysis it all comes down to a matter of subjective interpretation anyway."

In fact, though, the reality is that 95% of the apologetical questions are grouped around a set of basic questions that continue to be asked in almost every age, or at least asked by every age since the Enlightenment of the 18th century. However, few Christians are prepared with answers to what are overwhelmingly the same questions today as were asked 300 years ago. Illustrative of those basic questions are the following: "The New Testament text is corrupted and thus unreliable," or "miracles are impossible," or "the Trinity is contradictory and therefore irrational," or "science has disproven God."

The Centrality of Keeping Central What Is Central

> **Advocacy Principle No. 3**: Be able to explain your case in one sentence. As applied to the Christian advocate, make primary what Scripture makes primary (John 5:39; see also the Road to Emmaus at Luke 24:44)—which is Christ crucified for sinners and risen again for our justification.

Do not get derailed from the centrality of making the case for Christ. Illustrative of this is the following: One of us recently attended a seminar put on by a Texas-based evangelical

ministry that featured a lecture by a prominent evangelical figure on atheism that never mentioned Jesus Christ or
the resurrection once! We endured a similar fate at a recent
conference on Intelligent Design sponsored by a renowned
evangelical college—which managed to have a cadre of internationally recognized speakers who went an entire weekend
without mentioning Christ or the resurrection.[7]

Lawyers know the key point they must prevail on to
return a positive verdict. ("You must be absolutely clear
as to the theory of your case and keep it uppermost in
your mind **throughout the trial**." Cuthbert, *supra* at ft. 3,
p. 254—*emphasis added*).

Be prepared to jettison **all** other arguments if you find
them getting you onto tangents and distractions (e.g., proving theism in itself only sends people to hell as creationists,
or starting with the need for "a return to traditional family
values" devolves into fights over definitions and whether
"traditional family values" have been tried already and
found wanting).

This does not mean the advocate ignores legitimate
questions raised by their audience—they just don't let
such questions derail them from the central case for Christ.

We are reminded of the story about the hapless criminal defense counsel who explained to the jury that he had
5 powerful reasons why his client was innocent with number 5 being that his client just happened to be **dead** when
the crime occurred. The focused advocate would move up
reason 5 to reason number 1 and then promptly **sit down**
under the advocacy principle of "get to the heart of your case
and then sit down" or, put simply, "know when to shut your

---

7. This is particularly difficult for the authors to stomach seeing that
both are confessionally Lutheran, and our formal theological state-
ments all emphasize the utter centrality of the Gospel in doctrine
and practice.

mouth." If you detail at trial all the rest of the four defenses, you put those arguments on equal ground and devalue the key defense on which you win the case by burying it at argument number 5. It is like the lawyer who received a positive written tentative opinion from the court and then arrived for argument and proceeded to talk the Judge out of it!

What *is* our central message? Simply that Christ died for sinners and all listening qualify.

But first it is critical to explain the nature of the disease afflicting mankind and for which Christianity claims to provide a remedy.

The Reformers spoke of the problem this way: the presentation of the Law (that is, God's demands and our failure to obey God's Law) must always precede the declaration of the Gospel, otherwise Christ's death appears gratuitous and a strange remedy for a disease easily conquered by, say, moral reform. Luther is very clear on this: "We must know how to differentiate between them [Law & Gospel]. We must know what the Law is, and what the Gospel is. The Law commands and requires us to do certain things . . . the Gospel, however, does not preach what we are to do or to avoid. It sets up no requirements but reverses the approach of the Law, does the very opposite, and says: 'This is what God has done for you; He has let his Son be made flesh for you, has let him be put to death for your sake.' So, then there are two kinds of doctrine and two kinds of works, those of God and those of men . . . The Gospel teaches exclusively what has been given to us by God, and not—as in the case of the Law—what we are to do and give to God." *Luther's Works*, ed. Jaroslav Pelikan (Saint Louis: Concordia Publishing House, 1955), vol. 35, p. 162.[8]

---

8. Many Christians are reluctant to use the word "sin" anymore. Is this warranted? Hardly! The non-Christian can at least have "sin" explained as the failure to abide by his own moral code (see C. S. Lewis' "Mere Christianity" and "The Abolition of Man" on this subject).

Resurrecting the Resurrection
as the Central Christian Claim

What is the central claim? That Jesus died a real death, and rose from the dead 3 days later to attest to, or verify, what at first glance are mere "claims" by Jesus that belief in Him is the only means for the forgiveness of sins (see John 8:24: "If you do not believe in me you will die in your sins"). Paul's advocacy never compromises or avoids the centrality of the resurrection as a fact that can be proven by a preponderance of evidence under the civil standard, or "beyond a reasonable doubt to a moral certainty" under the criminal standard.

As for the significance of the resurrection, it is the center of every sermon in Acts. See, for example, 1 Corinthians 15:14—if Christ be not raised our faith is in vain and we are still in our sins. The resurrection distinguishes Christianity from all other religions and none have such a falsifiable factual event at their center.

We are reminded of the story by Duff Cooper in his biography of Talleyrand, the 18th century French politician. It so happened that Talleyrand attended a meeting where a new religion was being proposed by a one La Revelliere, who "bitterly hated" Christians and who suggested a new pseudo-philosophical religion be substituted in place of Christianity. He called this new religion "Theophilanthropy." La Revelliere read a long paper explaining this "novel system of worship" and when he had completed his presentation, he received congratulations from everybody in the room save for Talleyrand, who remarked as follows: "For my part I have only one observation to make. Jesus Christ, in order to found His religion, was crucified and rose again—you should have tried to do as much." Duff Cooper, *Talleyrand: A Biography* (New York: Fromm International Publishers, 1986), pp. 95–96.

It cannot be put more clearly: to every challenger to Christianity we simply echo Talleyrand and say "you should have tried to do as much."

The facticity of the resurrection, therefore, becomes utterly critical. We note here some sources to assist in being facile with the evidences for the resurrection: See Frank Morison, *Who Moved the Stone? The Evidence for the Resurrection* (London: Faber & Faber, 1944), esp. Chapter 1 entitled "The Book that Refused to be Written" where former skeptic Morison describes his intellectual journey to Christianity; see *The Resurrection Fact: Responding to Modern Critics*, eds. John Bombaro and Adam Francisco (Irvine: New Reformation Press, *2016*); see also the chapter entitled "The Resurrection of Jesus Christ on Trial" in *Making the Case for Christianity: Responding to Modern Objections*, eds. Korey Maas and Adam Francisco (St. Louis: Concordia Publishing House, 2014); Ross Clifford, *Leading Lawyers' Case for the Resurrection* (Edmonton: Canadian Institute for Law, Theology and Public Policy, 1996); Parton, *Religion on Trial* 2nd ed. (St. Louis: Concordia Publishing House, 2018); and books by John Warwick Montgomery including, *Faith Founded on Fact, Defending the Gospel in Legal Style, Evidence for Faith: Deciding the God Question, Christ our Advocate*, and *The Law Above the Law*.

The Advocate and Apologetics

First, a word about the two functions of "apologetics" or the defense of the Christian faith: the so-called "negative role" defined loosely as removing obstacles **and** its "positive role" in providing affirmative evidence.

The "negative" use of apologetics is often seen as its primary function—that is, "bringing down strongholds" and showing the logical and factual inadequacies within non-Christian positions. The negative use of apologetics is particularly attractive to: (1) pre-suppositional Calvinists (who see the Fall as precluding the unbeliever from ever getting the affirmative evidences right—but we must note here that if the unbeliever distorts the positive evidence for Christ, won't they distort the negative evidence too?); and (2) orthodox Lutherans (who see apologetics as inconsistent with Luther's explanation of the 3rd Article of the Creed that we "cannot by our own reason or strength believe in the Lord Jesus Christ or come to Him"). Many Lutherans actually function as presuppositional Calvinists when it comes to apologetics.

However, presenting positive evidence for the faith is critical and it is biblical.

We first note that refuting 1,847 other belief systems or isms does not prove the case for Christianity. The mere fact that you prove that the house next door to you has a rotted foundation does not *ipso facto* establish the solidity of the foundation of *your* home. In short, your religion may be wrong too.

One must at all costs resist the temptation to require the unbeliever to accept a substantive starting point or pre-supposition from you in order to present the case for Christ. The problem of requiring the Bible be accepted as inerrant or the "Gospel truth" or the "authority" before the conversation can go any further constitutes circular reasoning. One simply must start on common *epistemological* grounds with the skeptic.

As detailed in Part I herein, inductive logic seeks to **assume the least** and **prove the most**. This is how a trial operates. During a trial, what is called "Judicial Notice" may be taken of only uncontroverted matters. At best one can get Judicial Notice of uncontested pre-suppositions of **form** but never are pre-suppositions of **content** allowed into evidence by Judicial Notice. Thus, one can obtain Judicial Notice of the fact that May 19, 2024 was a Sunday. But one cannot get

Judicial Notice that on May 19, 2024, the defendant negligently crashed his car into the plaintiff's living room, since that is a disputed issue of fact and what the case is all about in the first place.

Van Tilian pre-suppositionalism requires that major presuppositions of substance or factual content be first accepted (e.g., the existence of God, the Bible as God's word etc.). The only presuppositions to be required for dialogue are the basic laws of logic, or so-called "presuppositions of form." Be prepared then to prove the case of Christianity once there is common ground as to the use of the basic laws of logic which everyone has to use or functioning in the world would be impossible.

A brief comment on tactics . . .

If you have 60 minutes with the unbeliever, spend 55 minutes on the positive evidence and center on the resurrection. Why? Because spending 55 minutes tearing down the skeptic's position will likely generate a defensive and reactionary response involving all kinds of psychological resistance for having their views attacked from the start—for the contrary approach, see Francis Schaefer who would reverse this order and spend 55 minutes on tearing down and challenging the world view of the skeptic and 5 minutes on positive apologetics or giving affirmative evidence for Christian belief.

The following are resources for handling the basic questions—Montgomery, *How do we know there is a God?*; Parton, *Religion on Trial*; *Objections Overruled: Answering Arguments Against Christianity* (St. Louis: Issues, etc.), Vol. 1 released in 2020, Vol. 2 in 2022, and Vol. 3 in 2024; see also R. C. Sproul, *Reasons to Believe*. Note: Students of apologetics might consider attending the International Academy of Apologetics which meets each July in Strasbourg, France (see www.apologeticsacademy.eu). The Academy is strongly in the evidentialist camp and its faculty and content emphasize the importance of the positive role or function of apologetics.

For the positive evidence for the Christian position, see Montgomery, *History, Law and Christianity*, and Parton, *Religion on Trial*.

We make reference here to an actual example of how to do apologetics. See Appendix A of this treatise, which resulted from 4 sessions of questions and answers with Dr. Montgomery at Patrick Henry College, and in which Mr. Parton acted as moderator and antagonist. At one moment in the pointed 4 hours of questions, Parton asked the following: "Aren't Eastern religious positions a much more attractive way to handle religious problems? Christianity has clearly been linked to destructive capitalism and war mongering and the thwarting of human rights, so why not move in the direction of Eastern answers: Buddhism, yoga and meditative religions and those kinds of approaches?" See Appendix A for the provocative response.

The Advocate and Setting out the Essential Case for Christianity in Legal Style

We highly recommend that the *logos* of Christianity be distilled to the following 5 points:

1. The New Testament Gospels are reliable historical documents. They are written either by eyewitnesses of the central events or close associates of eyewitnesses and circulated within the apostolic band. In short, these 4 sources (Matthew, Mark, Luke and John) are primary sources. See Frederick Kenyon, *Handbook to the Textual Criticism of the New Testament*; F. W. Hall, *Companion to Classical Texts*; John A. T. Robinson, *Redating the New Testament*; F. F. Bruce, *The New Testament Documents: Are they Reliable?*, as well as a current version of the Bruce thesis found in Jonathan Bernier, *Rethinking the Dates of the New Testament:*

The Evidence for Early Composition (Grand Rapids: Baker Books, 2022); see also J. W. Montgomery, *History, Law and Christianity*.

2. In these reliable historical documents Jesus claims to be nothing less than the Messiah (God enfleshed) prophesied in the Old Testament. John 1:1; 8:24 and 58; John 10:25–33; John 20:28; Mark 2. But anyone can *claim* to be God.

3. In all 4 Gospels, Christ's death and resurrection are described in great detail and take up a majority of each of the 4 books. Christ's death on the cross has been carefully examined by doctors and experts in Roman law and found to be exactly in harmony with those practices in the 1st century. See Journal of the AMA, March 21, 1986 for the article "On the Physical Death of Jesus Christ"; see also A. N. Sherwin-White, *Roman Society and Roman Law in the New Testament* (London: Oxford University Press, 1965).

4. Christ's resurrection proves His deity. If ever there was a place for worship, it is a man who wins the victory over death. Jesus just happens to be in the very best place to interpret the meaning of His own resurrection since He accomplished it!

5. If Christ is God, anything he says is true. He never criticizes Scripture or pits one verse against another but instead opines on the utter trustworthiness of every jot and tittle of the Old Testament (Matthew 5) and the coming New Testament (John 14 and 16).

This is the historical-legal argument that moves from the general "reliability" of the New Testament to Jesus Christ as God, and then Christ's own testimony grounds the ultimate complete reliability of Scripture. There may not be sufficient time to go through all 5 points systematically, but the individual parts of this outline are useful in their own right.

For example, mastering the evidence for point 1 lets the skeptic draw their own line from New Testament reliability to Jesus Christ as God in the flesh.

This legal case for Christ yields a totally reliable (yes, inerrant) Scripture as a secondary benefit! Jesus Christ is the best witness on the topic of the total trustworthiness of the Old and New Testaments. Why? Because, as noted, He rose from the dead verifying his claims to deity. As God his testimony is infinitely more reliable and infinitely more credible than say a 20th century German biblical critic.

Advocacy in the Forum of a Public Debate

The New Testament is replete with public defenses of the Gospel—see Paul (Acts 9), Stephen (Acts 7), Apollos (Acts 18), Peter (Acts 2), et al. We offer three thoughts to the Christian advocate who is venturing into a public debate.

First, know your opponent's case better than they do—study everything they wrote. Professor Montgomery has engaged in scores of public debates on the truth of Christianity. In one of those debates (Montgomery v. Thomas J. J. Altizer, death of God theologian), Montgomery quoted back to Altizer portions of Altizer's doctoral dissertation (which Montgomery went to great lengths to find and then to read) when Altizer was still a believer . . .

Second, whether in court or whether in a public debate, preparation is the best antidote for nervousness.

Third, reserve the *pathos* for the audience and *not* for your opponent during the debate.

Illustrative of this third principle is the debate between Francis Schaeffer and Bishop James Pike in January of 1968. Pike was totally vulnerable—a theological radical who denied the virgin birth and the trinity all the while wearing his clerical robes as an ordained bishop in the American Episcopal Church thus purposefully creating confusion as to what Christians actually believe, and who also participated in occult practices even using a medium through which he claimed to communicate with his dead son. The "debate" wasn't one. Schaeffer later corresponded with Pike up to Pike's death in 1969. They became friends and Schaeffer visited Pike at Pike's home. Fine. But unfortunately, the audience after the debate found no clear winner but agreed that both were very nice men.[9]

Conclusion: Don't Appear before God without a Lawyer!

Even the best human advocate needs a lawyer when appearing before God at the Great Assize. The accuser's claims in that day are painfully on target and we are guilty as charged. The whole world lies in a deep and dark bondage.

But the accuser is no match for Christ our Advocate . . . The Accuser has no standing to be in this court. He "who bore our sins on the Cross" has both standing to remit our transgressions and the jurisdictional power to do so. He has proven his advocacy by becoming man, living a perfect life in our stead, and suffering in our place.

We have the most competent defense counsel at our table . . . Indeed He is our "advocate with the Father" who gives us His righteousness for our sin and takes our death and gives us His life in exchange (1 John 2:1–2).

The best news ever is that He "ever lives to intercede (advocate) for us . . ." (Hebrews 7:25).

---

9. See "The Role of Public Debate in Apologetics," by Justice Dallas K. Miller, contained in *Tough-Minded Christianity: Honoring the Legacy of John Warwick Montgomery* (Nashville: B&H Publ. House, 2008), eds. William Dembski and Thomas Schirrmacher, pp. 452 ff. Justice Miller analyzes the tactics and strategy employed by Montgomery in nine public debates.

Suggested Readings

Books by John Warwick Montgomery:

Christ Our Advocate
Defending the Gospel in Legal Style
Evidence for Faith
Faith Founded on Fact
The Law Above the Law
The Shape of the Past
Where is History Going?

Books by Craig Parton:

Religion on Trial: Cross-Examining Religious Truth Claims
The Defense Never Rests: A Lawyer Among the Theologians
Richard Whately: A Man for All Seasons

Books by Lawyers on Advocacy:

Paul Bergman, *Trial Advocacy*
J. A. C. Brown, *Techniques of Persuasion: From Propaganda to Brainwashing*
Leslie Cuthbert, *365 Daily Advocacy Tips*
Keith Evans, *The Golden Rules of Advocacy*
Michael Hyam, *Advocacy Skills*
John H. Munkman, *The Technique of Advocacy*
R. K. Soonavala, *Advocacy: Its Principles and Practice*

Books by Lawyers and Judges on the Facticity of the Christian Faith:

Ethelbert Callahan, *The Lawyers of the Bible*

Herbert C. Casteel, *Beyond a Reasonable Doubt: A Judge's Verdict on the Case of Christian Faith*

Walter M. Chandler, *The Trial of Jesus from a Lawyer's Standpoint*

Pamela B. Ewen, *Faith on Trial: An Attorney Analyzes the Evidence for the Death and Resurrection of Jesus*

Lord Hailsham (Quintin McGarel Hogg), *The Door Wherein I Went*

Graeme Smith, *Was the Tomb Empty? A Lawyer Weighs the Evidence for the Resurrection*

APPENDIX A
Aren't Eastern Religious Options More Attractive Than Christianity?

[Dialogue between Craig Parton and Dr. John Warwick Montgomery at an Open Forum at Patrick Henry College]

Question posed by Craig Parton: *Aren't Eastern religious positions a much more attractive way to handle religious problems? Christianity has clearly been linked to destructive capitalism and war mongering on a global scale and the thwarting of human rights. Why not move in the direction of Eastern answers like Buddhism, yoga and an assortment of meditative religions?*

JWM: Well, a lot of those differences that you are referring to are really social differences. The fact that Christianity has operated in the Western context where, for example, capitalism has been so important economically—that sort of thing . . . But it is very hard to show that capitalism is the automatic product of Christianity.

It seems to me that if you're going to choose between Christianity and Eastern religions, you don't choose on the basis of the social conditions on which they operate. You choose on the basis of which offers evidence of truth.

And as we've tried to point out, Christianity does offer that objective evidence. We started here with that. Christianity offers objective evidence of its truth and therefore evidence that will justify our experiencing it, whereas the Eastern religions don't have any such objective evidence in their behalf whatsoever. My goodness, we don't have any contemporary information about Gautama Buddha at all. It's two centuries later, and even if we did it wouldn't make a lot of difference because Buddha simply declares the nature of the world. Why would we believe this when it contradicts what Christianity has to say and that is based directly on God Almighty coming directly to earth and demonstrating that He is indeed God in the flesh! Now maybe both of these religions are false but they can't both be true.

So, in this case, you need to check out the evidence. And this is not difficult in the case of the Eastern religions because there isn't any! There's only experience—there's nothing other than this.

In the case of Christianity there is objective evidence and therefore we ought to go in that direction. If we do get into the social side of this thing, then we see some pretty sobering considerations where the Eastern religions are concerned.

These religions have done nothing to ameliorate the social conditions where they have operated. And the reason for that is, for example, in Buddhism the Buddhist holds that all life is suffering and suffering is the product of desire. Not, mind you, desire for the bad but any desire! And so Buddhists do not make any efforts, they don't desire to clean up such things as the caste system . . . Gandhi said, even though he never became a Christian, that it was only in his Christian school that he came to realize how dreadful it was that there were outcasts and that the caste system operated. In short, the Eastern religions have been indifferent to human suffering in a way that has never been the case with Christianity.

Craig Parton: *Christianity, though, has a horrible track record of dealing with human suffering—it has actually promoted human suffering wherever it has gone.*

JWM: Oh piffle!

Parton: *Piffle?*

JWM: Piffle. I will not buy this. I will simply not buy this! Because as Alvin Schmidt has pointed out in his excellent work "Under the Influence," what Christianity has accomplished in civilization, in fact there has been no force in human history that has done more to alleviate human suffering than Christianity. Christianity is the source of the whole hospital-hospice tradition. In the first century it was only Christians who saved the lives of babies that were left on hillsides exposed because the Romans simply did not want to have them as babies. And the homes for orphans and my goodness, the abolition of slavery is the product of Christian influence. People like William Wilberforce and John Newton, the slave trader, who was converted and became one of the leading opponents of slavery, and on and on and on. The university tradition arose from the Christian Middle Ages. Public education arose from Luther's insistence that the Christian princes teach everybody so that everybody could read the Bible and become a literate person. And on and on and on . . . That's why I say "piffle."

APPENDIX B

The John Warwick Montgomery Lanier Theological Library Series Inaugural Lecture

By John Warwick Montgomery

Introduction

It is with the greatest pleasure that I offer this Inaugural Lecture in the Lanier Theological Library's proposed new lecture series in my honor.

The series has a major and a minor focus: *Evidential Apologetics* and *Juridical Apologetics*. I shall say just a word about both emphases before presenting my lecture proper.

Why apologetics in general and evidential apologetics in particular? The overarching reason is the nature of our world, characterized since at least the 18th century by increasing secularism. In this world, there is a plurality of conflicting religions and ideologies, and most people see them as matters of personal belief and emotional satisfaction. But they all purport to offer true (and conflicting) descriptions of the nature of the cosmos and the true values for human existence. A not insignificant number of these answers, when implemented (one thinks particularly of Islam) can leave a society devoid of human rights. It therefore becomes imperative to think in terms not of individual satisfaction but of *truth* in evaluating and choosing one's philosophy of life.

And here Christianity alone provides the solid, empirical base for a sound approach to the universe and a valid relationship with its Creator and Redeemer. 1 Corinthians 15:3-6: "I [the Apostle Paul] delivered unto you first of all that which I also received, how that Christ died for our sins according to the scriptures; and that he was buried, and that he rose again the third day according to the scriptures: and that he was seen of Cephas, then of the twelve: after that, he was seen by more than five hundred brethren at once; of whom the greater part remain unto this present."

This is not an aprioristic, analytically meaningless claim, as offered by the competing ideologies of modern secularism, but a factual assertion that can be supported by the very approach to evidence we use every day to distinguish fact from fancy.

I suggest that the 21st century Christian community (sadly including a good number of its evangelicals) has reduced biblical faith to cultic status by refusing to present the gospel as a matter of evidential truth. And I firmly believe that this reductionism is one of the most important reasons for the decline of our churches and the dechristianization of our modern societies.

One of the greatest ironies in the contemporary neglect of the apostolic command to "be ready always to give an answer [Gk., *apologia*] to every man who asks you a reason for the hope that is in you" (1 Peter 3:15) is that the discipline of systematic theology, at the heart of the Reformation theological curriculum, embraced three branches: dogmatics, ethics, *and apologetics*—and that at a time when the number of competing religious claims was immensely smaller than it is today. Classical theology was well aware that without solid reasons for the Christian hope, there is no epistemological grounding for the truth-claims of either scriptural doctrine or biblical morality.

But why a juridical or legal apologetic? Are not lawyers at best regarded as at the ethical level of used-car dealers or, at worst, as literally the devil's advocates (cf. the 1997 film starring Al Pacino and Keanu Reeves)? Leaving aside the ethical deficiencies of certain practitioners, one must recognize that the courts in every nation deal with the most intractable of social conflicts and decide them in principle by the marshaling and weighing of evidence.[1] The law is far more sophisticated in its understanding and treatment of facts than are philosophers or theologians (to say nothing of sociologists and *littérateurs*). It follows that if Christian faith, and not its opposing and mutually contradictory competing world-views, can pass the tests of juridical evidence, the non-Christian is left with the alternatives of jettisoning the law *per se* or taking Christian claims with utmost seriousness. A bad choice here is equivalent to an attempt to "stop the world so I can jump off"; a sound, mature choice leads to a world created by a loving God who was willing even to die for a rebel humanity and offers every person his Son as "the way, the truth, and the life."

A Montgomery lecture series under Lanier sponsorship can thus provide a hugely neglected avenue to church renewal and a significant vehicle for evangelizing a world in desperate need of eternal values.

And now: The Inaugural Lecture.

---

1. "The law is humanity's sanctuary, where we retreat from unreason. And humans need the law, because they need to believe there is some justice to their interactions, a justice that God or Fate or the Universe, call it what you like, will never provide on their own."—Scott Turow, *The Last Trial* (London: Mantle, 2020), p. 198.

Why Do Unbelievers Reject the Solid Evidences for Christian Truth?

The case for historic, biblical Christianity is overwhelmingly powerful. Creationism receives greater and greater support in the philosophical community and differs radically from the obscurantist efforts of atheists to argue that time and "mutation" somehow have the power to change empirical reality.[2] Historical evidences of the miraculous life and resurrection of Jesus Christ put Christianity in the category of analytical meaningfulness without significant parallel when compared with the other major world's religions, to say nothing of the cults and speculative philosophical isms.[3]

And yet, Christian apologetics so often find that unbelievers remain unconvinced when presented with evidence for gospel truth that, if offered as proof in secular areas, would be accepted without hesitation. Why is this so?

Let us begin by dismissing three inadequate answers.

Sin. Cosmically, this is most definitely the ultimate reason for unbelief and the rejection of the gospel. But we must not make the mistake of the ancients who explained rain simply as "the pissing of Zeus through the clouds." We need to understand, if possible, the earthly, empirical sources of dismissing good evidence in the case of revelational truth. This is especially so when such rejection on the part of the unbeliever is self-defeating to the extreme and takes no account of the cost of redemption to God himself or the love his incarnation and salvatory death displayed to every sinful human—including the person being evangelized.

---

2. See, e.g., J. P. Moreland (ed.), *Theistic Evolution: A Scientific, Philosophical, and Theological Critique* (Wheaton, IL: Crossway, 2017).

3. Cf. Richard Bauckham, *Jesus and the Eyewitnesses: The Gospels As Eyewitness Testimony* (2d ed.; Grand Rapids, MI: Eerdmans, 2017); and the present author's many works on this subject.

Predestination. We do not, to be sure, deny the efficacy of divine election or the monergism inherent in the biblical and Reformation teaching of *sola gratia*. But there is no way that the evangelist or apologist can determine that a given unbeliever has committed the unpardonable sin and is therefore in an eternally lost condition. Death—and nothing else—puts paid to one's eternal destiny.

Insensitive witness. Christians occasionally (and sadly) stand on the unbeliever's foot while witnessing to him or her and thereby create obstacles to personal commitment. But such insensitivity does not alter the force of the evidence for Christian truth. Our concern here is with rejection of Christ even when the case for accepting him is presented lovingly and effectively. "Ineffectiveness of counsel," though often a good ground of appeal in the criminal courts, will not wash when evaluating the rejection *per se* of the case for Christianity.

So, our initial question remains: *Why* do non-Christians sometimes reject out of hand the powerful evidence for the revelational truth of Christian proclamation?

Recent research in the legal field can provide much assistance in answering this question. We refer, in particular, to an analysis of "Why Clients Ignore Counsel's Advice."[4] This study isolates three major factors to explain client resistance to excellent legal advice provided by counsel—in remarkable disregard of the fact that the client is paying for that advice—*confirmation bias, the sunk cost fallacy,* and *delay and probability discounting.* Let us examine each of these considerations and apply the reasoning to the evangelistic and apologetical task.

---

4. Stephen D. Lott, Chit Yuen Yi, and Aaron D. Dumas, "The Science of Why Clients Ignore Counsel's Advice," *Washington Lawyer*, September/October 2020, pp. 33–37.

Confirmation bias:

As the term is typically used in the psychological literature, "confirmation bias" refers to "the seeking or interpreting of evidence in ways that are partial to existing beliefs, expectations, or a hypothesis in hand."[5] A legal example is the case of a client who, convinced that a competitor is trying to ruin his business, wants his lawyer to sue and rejects the lawyer's arguments against a lawsuit—even though there is no actionable proof of the competitor's damaging the client's operation, and a lawsuit would certainly fail and cost the client money.

Theologically, confirmation bias is often encountered in evangelism and apologetics when a Christian witness is presented to those of Jewish background, even when they are not practicing Jews or connected with a Synagogue. My beloved classics professor at Cornell University, the late Harry Caplan, fell into this category. When I tried to present the gospel and its truth-value to him, he simply refused to listen; his response was, "Stop right there; I am a Jew and that is all there is to it." All too often the Jew has grown up in a family or social environment where Christianity has always been denigrated, with stories of the medieval and modern persecutions of Jews by *goyim*. No account is taken of the difference between Christian treatment of Jews and treatment of them by non-Christian gentiles (e.g., the Nazis). Those with this confirmation bias uncritically accept what I have termed "Shirer's Re-Hitlerizing of

---

5. Raymond S. Nickerson, "Confirmation Bias: A Ubiquitous Phenomenon in Many Guises," 2/2 *Review of General Psychology* (1998), 175–220. See also: Margit E. Oswald and Stefan Grosjean, "Confirmation Bias," in Rüdiger F. Pohl (ed.), *Cognitive Illusions: A Handbook on Fallacies and Biases in Thinking, Judgement and Memory* (London: Psychology Press, 2004), pp. 79–96.

Luther," attributing to the Reformer a proleptic advocacy of the holocaust.[6]

The Sunk Cost Fallacy:

"The sunk cost effect is manifested in a greater tendency to continue an endeavor once an investment in money, effort, or time has been made . . . In a field study, customers who had initially paid more for a season subscription to a theater series attended more plays during the next 6 months, presumably because of their higher sunk cost in the season tickets."[7] In legal practice, a client not infrequently rejects solid advice from his or her attorney to jettison a legally questionable project simply because he has already expended much time, effort and money in pursuing it—even though continuing with it almost surely will entail grave legal consequences. The client dismisses good evidence and thereby "throws good money after bad" in order to achieve some kind of psychological consistency and justification for a prior bad decision.

One encounters this fallacy again and again in personal witness and in the apologetical defense of the faith. The unbeliever has become a member of atheistic societies and is highly regarded in those circles; or he/she has a long-term illicit sexual relationship going; or he/she has often appeared on television or radio debunking religious claims in general. The result is an irrational refusal to face good evidence: the cost would entail a change in conduct and serve

6. First published in the liberal theological journal *Christian Century*, and reprinted in Montgomery, *In Defense of Martin Luther* (Milwaukee: Northwestern Publishing House, 1970), pp. 142–49.

7. Hal R. Arkes and Catherine Blumer, "The Psychology of Sunk Cost," 35/1 *Organizational Behavior and Human Decision Processes* (February 1985), 124–40.

as an admission that one was *wrong* in one's earlier choices. One would lose face. Ego is at stake, so the easier path is to dismiss even the best of evidence.

Delay and Probability Discounting:

"Numerous behavioral studies have demonstrated that animals (including humans) tend to prefer delayed aversive consequences to immediate ones, *even if the delayed consequence is much worse than the immediate one* . . . In other words, people generally prefer to avoid a little bit of guaranteed pain now, even if it means they may experience a potentially larger amount of pain later."[8] General example: those who put off or refuse flu shots even though the result may well be a serious bout of flu later. Legal example: refusing one's lawyer's solidly based advice to reclassify certain "independent contractors" as regular employees; the client, though likely to face substantial future fines and loss of tax benefits, doesn't want to go to the lesser trouble and cost of reclassifications from independent contractor to employee "at least for now."

Non-Christians can and often do discount powerful evidence for Christian truth because, should they accept the gospel, they would need to make changes in their current lifestyle and/or practices. That present pain, however, is trivial when compared to the consequences of remaining in unbelief: a life lacking in ultimate purpose and divine guidance, followed by an eternity without benefit of God's love and grace.

* * *

---

8. Lott, Yi, and Dumas, *supra* at ft. 4, p. 35.

So, what can be done to counteract these fallacies and ratio-nalisations that imperil the soul?

Quite obviously, a kind and sensitive identification of the problem to the object of our witness and apologetic is essential. Often, the unbeliever is unaware of his or her reliance on considerations inimical to sound religious rea-soning. Analogies of a general, non-religious character may help—legal illustrations being particularly telling.

In another context, I have offered the following argu-ment. I believe that it can help here.

"As for biblical Christianity, the contrast [with Islam] could not be greater: there is the unqualified promise to believers in Romans 8:28 that 'all things work for good' on the basis of God's character as a loving Father—a promise that has been experientially and personally verified again and again in the lives of believers.

Let us express this point in formulaic . . . fashion.

Assuming that the standard of proof is satisfied (and *only* if that is the case):

> If one still hesitates in making
> a religious commitment, then

> Where C = legitimate commitment, B = concrete,
> empirical benefits promised by the faith, and
> E = entrance requirements to the faith,

$$C = B/E$$

Ergo: The less the entrance requirements and the higher the benefits, the more reason exists to commit to the evidence for a faith position already satisfying a high standard of proof . . .

We are arguing that, in contrast with competing reli-gious claims, acceptance of the gospel is a win-win situation.

Any doubts as to satisfying the standard of proof (and can this really be a problem, since the evidence level accords with the highest legal standard?) should be resolved in favor of the gospel, not against it. To argue in any other fashion is simply to declare: regardless of the evidence—and regardless of the maximal potential benefits available with minimal demands upon me—I prefer to remain the centre—the god—of my own life and universe. But that, as C. S. Lewis rightly observed, is the very definition of hell."[9]

To be sure, there is no magic formula to ensure that the case for Christianity will be evaluated seriously—much less for the achievement of successful conversion. That is the Holy Spirit's work. Our task is nothing more (*and nothing less!*) than to be responsible witnesses and effective conveyers of the "many infallible proofs"[10] of revelational truth.

---

9. Montgomery, "How Much Evidence To Justify Religious Conversion: Some Thoughts on Burden and Standard of Proof vis-à-vis Christian Commitment," 13/2 *Philosophia Christi* (2011), 339–50; reprinted in his *Defending the Gospel in Legal Style* (Bonn, Germany: Verlag fuer Kultur und Wissenschaft, 2017), pp. 21–33.

10. Acts 1:3.

APPENDIX C
Juridical Apologists
1600–2000 AD
A Bio-Bibliographical Essay

Philip Johnson

Presbyterian Theological Centre
Sydney, Australia

Since the seventeenth century, over one hundred and twenty Christian apologists have composed juridically (i.e., legal) styled apologetic texts. Juridical or jural apologetics may be defined as a style that employs either general legal principles or technical legal criteria in presenting a reasoned case for Christian belief. Apologists in this school are those who have been educated in the law and held positions as solicitors, barristers, judges, and law school lecturers. A few non-lawyers belong in this school because they follow jural methods, but space limitations preclude listing most of them. Thus, only ninety-two apologists appear in this bibliography.

What distinguishes juridical apologetics, as a distinct school of thought, is the use of jural analogies or metaphors that are applied in the defence of Scripture. Major analogies entail the concept of evidence, degrees of proof, and techniques for assessing eyewitnesses. Others include the interpretation of documents, the admissibility of ancient documents in court, judicial notice of accepted facts, and legal logic. Often the metaphors of a legal brief or a moot (mock trial) have been employed as a genre for the apologist's argument.

Most modern juridical apologists have operated in common-law based nations. Several have been scholars or practitioners of considerable renown who have exerted a lot of influence on subsequent popular apologetics. Remarkably, their contributions as a distinct school have gone unrecognised in the introductory textbooks on apologetics, even when such texts occasionally recognised in the introductory textbooks on apologetics, even when such texts occasionally mention one or more legal apologists. It is therefore hardly surprising that John Warwick Montgomery laments that it remains a neglected style. See his "Neglected Apologetic Styles: The Juridical and the Literary," in M. Bauman, D. Hall & R. Newman (Eds) *Evangelical Apologetics*, Camp Hill: Christian Publications, 1996.

This bibliography represents a start towards filling up the lacuna. It is arranged chronologically either by the date of the author's birth or where such data is lacking by the date of publication. Each author entry is numbered sequentially, and an alphabetical index of authors is supplied at the end. Bibliographical details have been checked against Religious Books 1876–1982, and the on-line catalogues of The British Library, Library of Congress, and the National Library of Canada.

[Note: See alphabetical list of scholars at end of article]

Legal Apologists 1600–2000

[1] **Hugo Grotius** [Huig De Groot] (1583–1645) the
Dutch jurist takes pride of place in modern juridical
apologetics. He is honoured as the father of international law particularly for his treatise *On The Law of
War and Peace* (1625). He studied law at the University
of Orleans and practised in Holland. Grotius was the
author of the first Protestant textbook in apologetics,
De Veritate Religionis Christianae (1627). It was originally composed in 1622 as a poem in Dutch and then
rewritten in Latin prose.

It was best known in English as *The Truth of
the Christian Religion* in six books, corrected and
illustrated with notes by Mr LeClerc, translated by
John Clarke, London: J. Knapton, 1711. The most
recent English edition was *True Religion*, Amsterdam:
Theatrum Orbis Terrarum/New York: Da Capo, 1971.
This was a photo reprint of the 1632 edition published
by R. Royston of London. On Grotius' life and influence see W. S. M. Knight, *The Life and Works of Hugo
Grotius*, London: Sweet & Maxwell, 1925.

[2] **Gottfried Wilhelm Leibniz** (1646–1716) was a
Lutheran theologian, philosopher and mathematician
who studied jurisprudence at Leipzig University. He
was a theistic rationalist who combined a mathe-
matical approach to epistemology and metaphysics
with empirical findings. He formulated arguments
for God's existence, and dealt with the problem of
evil. See his *Theodicy: Essays on the Goodness of
God, the Freedom of Man, and the Origin of Evil*,
trans. E. M. Huggard, London: Routledge & Kegan
Paul, 1951. *Monadology and Other Philosophical
Essays*, trans. H. Rose-Mont & D. J. Cook, Honolulu:
University of Hawaii Press, 1977. On Leibniz see

C. D. Broad, *Leibniz: An Introduction*, Cambridge: Cambridge University Press, 1975.

[3] **Thomas Sherlock** (1678–1761) was not a lawyer, but an Anglican Bishop. Sherlock was master of the Inner Temple church in London, which brought him into pastoral contact with members of the legal profession. He employed the device of a legal moot in his book *The Tryal of the Witnesses of the Resurrection of Jesus*, London: J. Baynes, 1729. Garland Publishing of New York reprinted Sherlock's Tryal, together with his Use and Intent of Prophecy in one volume in 1978.

Sherlock's moot assessed the apostolic witness to Jesus' resurrection and rendered a verdict in favour of the apostles. It was conceived as a rebuttal to the Cambridge Deist Thomas Woolston (1670–1731). Woolston had composed *Discourse on the Miracles of Our Saviour, In View of the Present Contest between Infidels and Apostates* (1727–29), wherein he found several gospel accounts of miracles to be fraudulent. Sherlock's Tryal stimulated six sceptical treatises from Peter Annet (1693–1769). Sherlock replied to Annet in *The Sequel of the Tryal of the Witnesses of the Resurrection of Jesus Christ* (1749). On Sherlock's life and work see Edward Carpenter, *Thomas Sherlock 1678–1761*, London: SPCK, 1936.

[4] **William Webster** (1689–1758) was not a lawyer but an eccentric theologian and prolific author. Webster wrote two brief treatises that have a legal flavour to them: *The Credibility of the Resurrection of Christ upon the Testimony of the Apostles* (1735) and *The Fitness of the Witnesses of the Resurrection of Christ* (1781). Both works were reprinted in The Simon Greenleaf Law Review, Vol. 6 (1986–87).

[5] **Joseph Butler** (1692–1752) studied law and divinity at Oriel College, Oxford. In 1736 Butler wrote

The Analogy of Religion Natural and Revealed to the Constitution and Course of Nature, London: George Bell, 1902. Butler used legal analogies with respect to the apostolic witnesses, and argued for a cumulative case based on both "direct and circumstantial evidence" for the truth of Christianity, particularly with regard to miracle and fulfilled prophecy in Jesus' ministry. See Part 2, chapter 7, pp. 285 & 292. Cf. Albert E. Baker, *Bishop Butler*, London: SPCK/New York & Toronto: Macmillan, 1923.

[6] **William Warburton** (1698–1779) was a lawyer and then served as a preacher to barristers at Lincoln's Inn (1746). Warburton's best-known apologia was a six-volume work entitled *The Divine Legation of Moses* (1737–1741). In 1768 he established by a testamentary bequest The Warburton Lecture which is devoted to the defence of revealed religion, especially Christianity. See Arthur William Evans, *Warburton and the Warburtonians*, London & Oxford: Oxford University Press, 1932.

[7] **Gilbert West** (1703–1756) served as clerk to the Privy Council. His apologia was entitled *Observations on the History and Evidence of the Resurrection of Jesus Christ*, London: R. Dodsley at Tully's Head, Pall Mall, 1747 and reprinted in Boston: J. Loring, 1834. It was composed as a rebuttal to Annet's *The Resurrection of Jesus Consider'd* (1744). West's book earned him the Doctor of Laws degree from Oxford (1748). See the *Dictionary of National Biography*.

[8] **William Paley** (1743–1805) had a life-long interest in the law and served as a justice of the peace. Paley's *A View of the Evidences of Christianity* (1794) occasionally reflects a legal turn of phrase. On Paley see M. L. Clarke, *Paley: Evidences for the Man*, Toronto: University of Toronto Press/London: SPCK, 1974.

[9] **John Hewson** (c.1768–) was not a lawyer but a pastor. He wrote *Christ rejected: or, The Trial of the Eleven Disciples of Christ, in a Court of Law and Equity, as Charged with Stealing the Crucified Body of Christ out of the Sepulchre. Humbly Dedicated to the Whole Nation of the Jews, which are Scattered Abroad on the Face of the Earth: and to Deists of Modern Times. Designed, Also, as a Help to Wavering Christians.* This was released under the pseudonym of Captain Onesimus. J. Bakestraw released the first edition in Philadelphia (1832), and R. E. Horner in Princeton reprinted it (1835).

  The Library of Congress indexes it under the subject heading "Jesus Christ—resurrection," which along with the lengthy title suggests it is apologetic in nature. However a description from an antiquarian dealer characterises it as a mystical work that includes devotional illustrations provoked by the 1830 exhibition of Benjamin West's picture "Christ rejected."

[10] **Lord Lyndhurst** [John Singleton Copley] (1772–1863) was Solicitor-General of England in 1819, Attorney-General in 1824, and thrice served as Lord Chancellor of England. Lyndhurst never published an apologia during his lifetime, but a written account of his Christian belief was discovered amongst his papers. He wrote, "I know pretty well what evidence is; and, I tell you, such evidence as that for the Resurrection has never broken down yet." Different apologists, such as Josh McDowell and Wilbur Smith, have cited these remarks. The original source is probably Sir Theodore Martin, *A Life of Lord Lyndhurst From Letters and Papers in Possession of his Family*, London: John Murray, 1883.

[11] **Henry Lord Brougham** (1778–1868) served as Lord Chancellor of England. He studied law at the

University of Edinburgh and was admitted to the
bar in Lincoln's Inn (1803). He sat in the Supreme
Court of Appeal and in the judicial committee of
the Privy Council. Lord Brougham's contribution
to apologetics consisted of editing and annotating
an edition of Paley's works, as well as writing his
own text *A Discourse of Natural Theology Showing
the Nature of the Evidence and the Advantages of the
Study*, London: Charles Knight/New York: William
Jackson, 1835. Brougham stated, "Upon testimony,
then, all Revelation must rest. Every age but the
one in which the miracles were wrought, and every
country but the one that witnessed them—indeed,
all people of that country itself save those actually
present—must receive the proofs which they afford
of Divine interposition upon the testimony of eyewitnesses, and of those to whom eye-witnesses told
it." (pp. 172–173). On Brougham see *The Dictionary of
National Biography*.

[12] **Thomas Hartwell Horne** (1780–1862) is best remembered as a librarian and Bible commentator, but
he was also for a time a clerk to a barrister. He was
ordained in the Church of England and later worked
at the British Museum. Horne authored some forty
books in apologetics and bibliography. The American
legal apologists Simon Greenleaf and Francis Lamb
relied on Horne's *Introduction to the Study of the Holy
Scriptures*, which uses the legal method of harmoni-
zation of Biblical narratives. On Horne see Douglas'
New International Dictionary of the Christian Church.

[13] **Daniel Webster** (1782–1852) was one of the most
distinguished legal authorities in the early history
of the United States of America. Apologists such as
Howard Hyde Russell (see below at number 34) quote
Webster on his Christian convictions, but invariably

fail to supply any bibliographical references. Webster evidently gave an apologia for Christianity in the course of a case before the US Supreme Court in 1844. It was concerned with a bequest that established a school for white male orphans. The bequest stipulated that no clergy were permitted under any circumstances to enter the college grounds. Webster argued the Will's bequest violated the public policy of Pennsylvania to foster religious sentiment. See Daniel Webster, *A defence of the Christian religion and of the religious instruction of the young; delivered in the Supreme Court of the US, February 10, 1844 in the case of Stephen Girard's Will*, New York: M. H. Newman, 1844. On Webster see the *Dictionary of American Biography*.

[14] **André Marie Jean Jacques Dupin** (1783–1865) was a prolific French legal author. The Library of Congress lists thirty-one titles in French. Of interest to apologists is his work first published in French as *Jésus devant Caïphe et Pilate*, and translated as *The Trial of Jesus before Caiaphas and Pilate*. Being a refutation of Mr. Salvador's chapter entitled "The Trial and Condemnation of Jesus," Boston: C. C. Little & Brown, 1839. American legal apologist Simon Greenleaf relied on Dupin in his own work.

[15] **Simon Greenleaf** (1783–1853) must be regarded as the pivotal figure in juridical apologetics. Greenleaf trained for the law in Maine, and in 1833 became Royall Professor of Law at Harvard. Greenleaf wrote *A Treatise on the Law of Evidence*, which became a standard authoritative text in nineteenth century American jurisprudence. Greenleaf's apologetic work, which remains in print today, was published in 1846 as *An Examination of the Testimony of the Four Evangelists by the Rules of Evidence Administered in*

Courts of Justice, with an Account of the Trial of Jesus.
Now available as *The Testimony of the Evangelists*,
Grand Rapids, MI: Baker, 1984. This text has influenced many subsequent juridical apologists. See the
Dictionary of American Biography. Cf. Ross Clifford,
Leading Lawyers' Case for the Resurrection, Edmonton:
Canadian Institute for Law, Theology & Public Policy,
1996.

[16] **Thomas Erskine** (1788–1870) was a Scottish
lawyer and lay theologian. He did not follow the
traditional apologetic line of arguing from prophecy and miracles, but rather wrote an apologetic
for the inner spiritual life entitled, *Remarks on the
Internal Evidence for the Truth of Revealed Religion*,
Edinburgh: Waugh & Innes, 1820. Dulles comments
that "as a testimony to the inner life of a deeply
convinced Christian, Erskine's *Internal Evidence* is
not unimpressive" (*A History of Apologetics*, Eugene:
Wipf & Stock, 1999, p. 171).

[17] **Charles Grandison Finney** (1792–1875) is best
remembered both for his role as an evangelist and for
his advocacy of the abolition of slavery. Before Finney
became an evangelist he trained as a lawyer in New
York. He later characterised his transfer from law
to evangelism as the Lord putting him on a retainer to
plead God's cause. Although principally an evangelist
and theologian, Finney did compose some apologetic
material. See Charles G. Finney, *Charles G. Finney:
An Autobiography*, London & New York: The
Salvation Army Book Depot, 1903.

[18] **Phineas Bacon Wilcox** (1798–1863) was a Yale graduate in law who practised in Columbus Ohio from
1824. He served as a chancery lawyer, was prosecuting attorney reporter for the Supreme Court of Ohio,
and was a United States commissioner. Wilcox was

the author of seven legal texts and wrote a 48 page apologetic text entitled *A Few Thoughts by a Member of the Bar, Occasioned by a Request From a Brother in the Same Profession* (Columbus OH: T. B. Cutler, 1836; republished New York: American Tract Society, 1860).

[19] **Mark Hopkins** (1802–1887) was a popular theologian, philosopher and educator who had a lifelong interest in the law. Hopkins' book *Evidences of Christianity* (1846) went through successive printed editions up to 1909. Hopkins relied on Paley and Horne and his discussion of eyewitness testimony has a legal flavour to it. As an apologist Hopkins' contribution might be considered as a nineteenth century equivalent to Josh McDowell. See Mark Hopkins, *Evidences of Christianity: Lectures Before the Lowell Institute, January 1844*, Rev. Ed. Boston: T. R. Marvin, 1876. On Hopkins see *American Authors 1600–1900*.

[20] **Charles Robert Morrison** (1819–1893) practised as a lawyer in New Hampshire and was the author of four legal textbooks. Morrison wrote *The Proofs of Christ's Resurrection; From a Lawyer's Standpoint*, Andover MA: Warren F. Draper, 1882. This monograph is based on a series of articles published in the *New Hampshire Journal* and in the *Vermont Chronicle* between March 5, 1881 and April 1, 1882. In the preface he stated that "to all questions of evidence which arise, the author applies legal principles and presumptions derived from experience and constantly acted upon in courts of justice" (p. 4).

[21] **Francis Wharton** (1820–1889) graduated in law from Yale in 1839 and was admitted to the Philadelphia bar in 1843. Wharton wrote several legal textbooks some of which are still in print, including *A Treatise on the Criminal Law of the United States* (1846). He was ordained in the Episcopal Church

in 1862, and served as Professor of Canon Law at the Episcopal Theological School in Cambridge, Massachusetts (1871–1881). Wharton did not compose an apologia per se, but did write a very important essay linking jurisprudence to apologetics, see "Recent Changes in Jurisprudence and Apologetics," *The Princeton Review*, 2/1 (July–December 1878) pp. 149–168. On Wharton see *The Columbia Encyclopedia*, 6th Ed, and also John Bassett Moore, *Brief Sketch of the Life of Francis Wharton*, Philadelphia, n.p. 1891.

[22] **Oliver Mowat** (1820–1903) was a distinguished Canadian lawyer and politician. He was admitted to the bar in 1841, practised law in the towns of Kingston and Toronto, became a Queen's Counsel in 1855, and later became a bencher of the Law Society of Upper Canada. He served as premier of Ontario from 1872–1896 and in 1897 became Lieutenant Governor of Ontario. Mowat wrote two small apologetic texts: *Christianity and Some of its Evidences: an Address*, Toronto: Williamson & Co, 1890. *Christianity and Its Influences*, Toronto: Hunter Rose, 1898. On Mowat see *The Dictionary of Christianity in America*.

[23] **Edmund H. Bennett** (1824–1898) was born in Vermont and admitted to the bar in 1847. He was appointed a judge in 1858 and lectured at Harvard. He was a prolific author of over one hundred texts. He delivered an apologetic lecture, which was then published posthumously as *The Four Gospels from a Lawyer's Standpoint*, Boston & New York: Houghton, Mifflin & Co, 1899. It was reprinted in *The Simon Greenleaf Law Review* Vol. 1 (1981–82), and the journal also includes two biographical profiles. Cf. Clifford, *Leading Lawyers' Case for the Resurrection*, pp. 15–27.

APPENDIX C

[24] **Francis Jones Lamb** (c.1824–c.1914) began to practise law in 1857 in Dane County, Madison, Wisconsin. At ninety years of age he co-wrote with William P. Morris, *Reminiscences of the Bench and Bar of Dane County*, Madison WI: Dane County Bar Association, c. 1914, 42pp. Lamb's apologetic work was *Miracle and Science: Bible Miracles Examined By The Methods, Rules and Tests of the Science of Jurisprudence as Administered To-day in Courts of Justice*, Oberlin OH: Bibliotheca Sacra Co, 1909. Lamb dealt with the problem of miracles throughout the Bible and employed technical arguments concerning ancient documents and eyewitness testimony.

[25] **Ethelbert Callahan** (1829–1918) *The Lawyers of the Bible. A Lecture delivered before the Indiana University School of Law*, January 23, 1911, Indianapolis, Indiana: Hollenbeck Press, 1912.

[26] **Charles Carroll Morgan** (1832–1918) was a lawyer in New Hampshire. His apologetic work was *A Lawyer's Brief on The Atonement*, Boston: Fort Hill Press, 1910. Although primarily treating the biblical teaching on atonement, Morgan does set out an argument for God's existence, the testimony for Jesus' death and resurrection, and uses the legal principle of harmonisation when treating Scripture.

[27] **Alexander Taylor Innes** (1833–1912) was a Scottish advocate best known for his *The Law of Creeds in Scotland. A Treatise on the Relation of Churches in Scotland Established and Not Established to the Civil Law*, Edinburgh: W. Blackwood, 1867. Of interest to legal apologists is *The Trial of Jesus Christ: A Legal Monograph*, Edinburgh: T & T Clark, 1899.

[28] **Everett Pepperell Wheeler** (1840–1925) wrote six legal textbooks. His apologetic work was *A Lawyer's Study of the Bible; Its Answers to the Questions of Today*, New York: Fleming Revell, 1919.

[29] **Robert Anderson** (1841–1918) studied law at Trinity College, Dublin, and became a barrister in Dublin and London. Anderson dealt with Bible prophecy, the creation-evolution controversy and higher criticism. Three relevant works include *A Doubter's Doubts about Science and Religion*, 3rd Ed. Glasgow & Edinburgh: Pickering & Inglis, 1924. *The Coming Prince*, 19th Ed. Grand Rapids: Kregel, 1975. *The Bible and Modern Criticism*, 5th Ed. London: Hodder & Stoughton, 1905. On Anderson's life see A. P. Moore-Anderson, *Sir Robert Anderson and Lady Agnes Anderson*, London: Marshall, Morgan & Scott, 1947. Cf. Clifford, *Leading Lawyers' Case for the Resurrection*, pp. 56–69.

[30] **Edward Wingate Hatch** (1852–1924) composed around 1892 *The Trial and Condemnation of Christ as a Legal Question*, New York: Knickerbocker, 1892.

[31] **Charles Edmund De Land** (1854–1935) *The Mis-Trials of Jesus*, Boston: R. G. Badger, 1914.

[32] **George Henry Pendarvis** (1854–1923) *The Living Witness: A Lawyer's Brief for Christianity*, St. Louis: B. Herder, 1912.

[33] **John Ford Whitworth** (1854–1929) wrote seven legal textbooks, and his apologia was *Legal and Historical Proof of the Resurrection of the Dead with an Examination of the Evidence in the New Testament*, Harrisburg: Publishing House of the United Evangelical Church, 1912.

[34] **Howard Hyde Russell** (1855–1946) wrote *A Lawyer's Examination of the Bible*, New York: Fleming Revell, 1893. This text went through seven editions, the last of which was published in 1935 by The Bible Bond in Westerville, Ohio.

[35] **Thomas Welburn Hughes** (1858–1943) *Was Jesus Guilty? Or, The legal Aspects of the Trial and Condemnation of Jesus*, Topeka: Voiland, 1927.

[36] **Philip Mauro** (1859–1952) was a New York lawyer who contributed some essays to *The Fundamentals*. His legal apologetic was *Evolution at the Bar*, Boston: Hamilton, 1922.

[37] **William Jennings Bryan** (1860–1925) was the outspoken apologist for creation at the John Scopes trial of 1925. See William Jennings Bryan, *The Last Message of William Jennings Bryan*, New York & Chicago: Fleming Revell, 1925.

[38] **John Armstrong Chaloner** (1862–1935) was an eccentric millionaire and New York lawyer. He composed *A Brief for the Defence of the Unequivocal Divinity of the Founder of Christianity as the Son of Jehovah*, New York: Palmetto, 1924.

[39] **Walter Nicholas Carroll** (1863–) *A Lawyer's Story of the Simple Gospel*, with an introduction by Dr Richard Burton, Minneapolis, n.p. 1927.

[40] **George Washington Thompson** (1864–1951) was Professor of Law at the University of Florida. He wrote *The Trial of Jesus Christ: A Judicial Review of the Law and Facts of the World's Most Tragic Court Room Trial*, Indianapolis: Bobbs-Merrill, 1927.

[41] **Walter Marion Chandler** (1867–1935) was a New York lawyer who wrote *The Trial of Jesus from a Lawyer's Standpoint*, 2 Vols. New York: Empire Publishing, 1908. Reprinted in New York by Federal Book, 1925. Reprinted in Atlanta by Harrison, 1956 & 1976. Reprinted in New York by W. S. Hein, 1983.

[42] **Edwin Taliaferro Wellford** (1870–1956) appears to have composed two apologias on Jesus' trial: *The Lynching of Jesus; A Review of the Legal Aspects of the Trial of Christ*, Newport News: Franklin Printing, 1905. *Crime and Cure; A Review of this Lawless Age and the Mistrial of Christ*, Boston: Stratford, 1930.

[43] **Edward Deming Lucas** (1878–1954) was a lawyer in Virginia. He wrote a slightly autobiographical work

Virginia Justice: Its Cause and Cure (1945). His apologetic text was *The Logic and Reason in Christianity.
A Brief by a Lawyer*, New York & London: Fleming Revell, 1945.

[44] An anonymous work by a **Nova Scotian judge** was published in London in 1878. The British Library's online catalogue furnishes these details: [anon.] *A Quaint Old Nova Scotian Judge's View of the Roman Governor's Question, "What is Truth?"* London: W. Ridgway, 1878.

[45] **Irwin Helffenstein Linton** (1879–1962) was a lawyer who practised in Washington DC. He wrote two apologetic works: *A Lawyer Examines the Bible*, Boston: W. A. Wilde, 1943, 300 pp. Reissued in 1977 by Baker. Originally released as 204 pp text, *A Lawyer and the Bible*, New York & London: Harper, 1929, and as *A Legal Man and the Bible*, London & Edinburgh: Marshall, Morgan & Scott, 1930. Linton's other book was *The Sanhedrin Verdict*, New York: Loizeaux, 1943.

[46] **Claude Watson Rowe** (1883–1960) served as a lawyer in New York and North Carolina. He wrote a legal textbook *How and Where Lawyers Get Practice* (1950), and compiled a curious book of minor apologetic value entitled *The Lawyers' Proof of the Hereafter*, Chicago, Philadelphia & Toronto: John C. Winston, 1938. Rowe's text focuses on the question, "What is the best evidence as to whether there is a hereafter or not?" Rowe submitted this question to over 600 colleagues: lawyers, law clerks, judges, law professors and so forth. The answers are sorted into 45 topics such as God, prayer, Bible, reincarnation, spiritualism, heaven, hell etc. The replies come from Christians, Jews, and agnostics. Rowe's theological views appear to be Unitarian. He stated, "My chief reason for making this book a symposium of the opinions of lawyers is that the legal mind is peculiarly fitted to weigh and analyze evidence . . . I felt that proof based upon the judicial,

unprejudiced, and critical survey of the evidence the legal minds would give it would be far more convincing than proof derived from opinions based on more personal grounds." (p. vii).

[47] **Walter Campbell Witcher** (1887–1965) *Legal Proof; Being an Answer to Thomas H. Huxley and Other Skeptics Demands for Legal Proof of the Resurrection of Christ from the Dead, and Containing Pilate's Official Verification of the Same.* Fort Worth: Christian Forum, 1937.

[48] **Frank John Powell** (1891–1971) served as both a barrister and magistrate in England. Powell wrote *The Trial of Jesus Christ*, London: Paternoster, 1948/Grand Rapids: Eerdmans, 1949.

[49] **Clarence Bartlett** (1895–1977) practised law in Kentucky from 1921–1938, and then served as a Circuit Judge. He wrote *As A Lawyer Sees Jesus: A Logical and Historical Analysis of the Scriptural and Historical Record*, New York: Greenwich, 1960.

[50] **J. C. Mabry (d. 1944)**, *A Legal View of the Trial of Christ*, Cincinnati: Standard, 1895.

[51] **Britton H. Tabor (d. 1901)**, *Skepticism Assailed; or, Foundations of Faith; Being a Trained Lawyer's Investigation of the Truth of the Bible and Divinity of Jesus*, St. Louis: Planet Publishing, 1896.

[52] **Andrew Bevins**, *The Trial and Conviction of Jesus Christ from a Legal Standpoint*, Omaha: Douglas Printing, 1898.

[53] **Joseph Evans Sagebeer** was a Philadelphia lawyer who edited a periodical called *The Optimist* (1903) and wrote *A First Book in Christian Doctrines*, Philadelphia: American Baptist Society, 1903. Sagebeer's apologia was *The Bible in Court: The Method of Legal Inquiry Applied to the Study of the Scriptures*, Philadelphia: J. B. Lippincott, 1900.

Reprinted in Littleton, Colorado by Fred B. Rothman, 1988.

[54] **Thomas Frew Wilson**, *The Trial of Jesus of Nazareth from an Historical and Legal Standpoint*, New York: T. Whittaker, 1906.

[55] **Lord Hailsham** [Quintin McGarel Hogg] (1907–2001) served as Lord Chancellor of England. Hailsham's spiritual autobiography has some apologetic chapters, *The Door Wherein I Went*, London: Collins, 1975. Hailsham also makes pertinent remarks at the conclusion of his *A Sparrow's Flight: Memoirs*, London: Collins, 1990. Cf. Clifford, *Leading Lawyers' Case for the Resurrection*, pp. 70–81.

[56] **W. D. Webb** was a judge who wrote *The Trial of Jesus Christ. A Lecture in Two Parts*, Atchison: Schauer & Burbank, 1907.

[57] **Norman Anderson** [James Norman Dalrymple Anderson] (1908–1994) studied law at Cambridge and became a leading expert on Islamic jurisprudence. He taught at the University of London and was Director of the Institute of Advanced Legal Studies. His apologetic works include: *The Evidence for the Resurrection*, Leicester: InterVarsity Press, 1965. *A Lawyer Among the Theologians*, London: Hodder & Stoughton, 1973. *The Fact of Christ: Some of the Evidence*, Leicester: InterVarsity Press, 1979. *Christianity and World Religions*, Leicester: InterVarsity Press, 1984. *Jesus Christ: The Witness of History*, Leicester: InterVarsity Press, 1985. *Islam in the Modern World*, Leicester: Apollos, 1990. His autobiography, *An Adopted Son*, Leicester: InterVarsity Press, 1985. Cf. Clifford, *Leading Lawyers' Case for the Resurrection*, pp. 82–108.

[58] **James M. Rollins**, *The Arrest, Trial and Conviction of Jesus Christ from a Lawyer's Standpoint*, St. Louis: Hughes Printing, circa 1951.

[59] **Lionel Luckhoo** (1914–1997) was a barrister in
      Guyana and England, and served as a judge of the
      Supreme Court of Guyana. Upon retirement he estab-
      lished Luckhoo Ministries in Texas. He co-wrote an
      apologetic novel with John R. Thompson, *The Silent
      Witness*, Nashville: Thomas Nelson, 1995. He also
      composed several pamphlets such as *What is Your
      Verdict*; *Prophecy*; *The Quran is not the word of God*;
      The Question Answered. Cf. Clifford, *Leading Lawyers'
      Case for the Resurrection*, pp. 109–119.

[60] **Gleason L. Archer** (1916–2004) was an Old
      Testament scholar, but who also earned an LLB.
      Archer uses the legal principle of harmonisation in
      his *Encyclopedia of Bible Difficulties*, Grand Rapids:
      Zondervan, 1982.

[61] **Stephen D. Williams** was a lawyer in Detroit and
      wrote *The Enemies of Columbia* (1896) and a work
      on economics (1897). His apologetic text was a moot
      trial published as *The Bible in Court or Truth vs. Error:
      A Brief for the Plaintiff*, Dearborn: Dearborn Book
      Concern, 1925.

[62] **Val Grieve** (1926–1998) was a solicitor who practised
      in Manchester. He wrote *Your Verdict on the Empty
      Tomb*, Bromley: OM Publishing, 1988. *The Trial of
      Jesus*, Bromley: STLBooks/Leicester: InterVarsity
      Press, 1990.

[63] **Clarrie Briese** (1930–) was a barrister and served
      as Chief Magistrate of New South Wales. He gave an
      address to the Lawyer's Christian Fellowship entitled
      "Witnesses to the Resurrection—Credible or Not," on
      March 11, 1987, portions of which are reproduced in
      Clifford, *Leading Lawyers' Case for the Resurrection*,
      pp. 132–135. His articles include: "An Open Mind,"
      Australian Presbyterian, July 1999, p. 28. "Monkeying
      About," *Australian Presbyterian*, September 1999,

pp. 24–25. "Darwin's unholy ghost," *Australian Presbyterian*, October 1999, pp. 19–21. "Doctrine of death," *Australian Presbyterian*, November 1999, pp. 18–19. "Is theistic evolution credible?" *Australian Presbyterian*, December 1999, pp. 22–23. "The Verdict," *Australian Presbyterian*, April 2000, pp. 5–6.

[64] **John Warwick Montgomery**, (1931–) is a versatile scholar and apologist, holding ten earned degrees including three in law. He taught jurisprudence at the Simon Greenleaf School of Law and the University of Luton. Relevant legal apologetic publications include: (Ed) *Jurisprudence: A Book of Readings*, Strasbourg: International Scholarly Publications, 1974. "Legal Reasoning and Christian Apologetics," *Christianity Today*, February 14, 1975, pp. 71–72. *The Law Above the Law*, Minneapolis: Bethany, 1975. *Law & Gospel*, Oak Park: Christian Legal Society, 1978. Reprinted in 1995 by the Canadian Institute for Law, Theology & Public Policy. "Testamentary Help in Interpreting the Old and New Testaments," *Christianity Today*, May 5, 1978, pp. 54–55. "Jesus Takes the Stand: An Argument to Support the Gospel Accounts," *Christianity Today*, April 9, 1982, pp. 26–27. "The Marxist Approach to Human Rights: Analysis & Critique," *Simon Greenleaf Law Review*, Vol. 3 (1983–84) pp. 1–202. *Human Rights & Human Dignity*, Grand Rapids: Zondervan, 1986. Reprinted in 1995 by Canadian Institute for Law, Theology & Public Policy. "Law and Justice," in Kenneth S. Kantzer (Ed) *Applying the Scriptures*, Grand Rapids: Zondervan, 1987, pp. 299–314. Reprinted in Michael Bauman & David Hall (Eds) *God & Caesar*, Camp Hill: Christian Publications, 1994, pp. 319–341. *Giant in Chains: China Today and Tomorrow*, Milton Keynes: Word, 1994. *Law and Morality: Friends or Foes?* London:

University of Luton, 1994. "Legal Hermeneutics and
the Interpretation of Scripture," in Michael Bauman &
David Hall (Eds) *Evangelical Hermeneutics*, Camp Hill:
Christian Publications, 1995, pp. 15–29. *Christians
in the Public Square: Law, Gospel & Public Policy*,
Edmonton: Canadian Institute for Law, Theology &
Public Policy, 1996. *The Repression of Evangelism in
Greece: European litigation vis-à-vis a Closed Religious
Establishment*, Lanham: University Press of America,
2001. Montgomery's legal apologia is treated in
Clifford, *Leading Lawyers' Case for the Resurrection*,
pp. 28–40. Atheist lawyer Richard Packham presents a
"Critique of John Warwick Montgomery's Arguments
for the Legal Evidences for Christianity" at infidel.org/
library/modern/richard-packham-montgmry

[65] **Philip E. Johnson** (1940–2019) teaches law at the
University of California at Berkeley. His works
include *Darwin on Trial*, Downers Grove: InterVarsity
Press, 1991. *Reason in the Balance: The Case Against
Naturalism in Science, Law and Education*, Downers
Grove: InterVarsity Press, 1995. *Defeating Darwinism
by Opening Minds*, Downers Grove: Inter-Varsity
Press, 1997. *Objections Sustained: Subversive Essays
on Evolution, Law and Culture*, Downers Grove:
InterVarsity Press, 1998. *The Wedge of Truth: Splitting
the Foundations of Naturalism*, Downers Grove:
InterVarsity Press, 2000. Idem & Denis O. Lamoureux,
Darwinism Defeated? Vancouver: Regent College, 1999.

[66] **Pamela Binnings Ewen** (1944–) is a Texas lawyer
specialising in corporate finance. She has written
*Faith on Trial: An Attorney Analyzes the Evidence
for the Death and Resurrection of Jesus*, Nashville:
Broadman & Holman, 1999.

[67] **David K. Breed**, *The Trial of Christ from a Legal and
Scriptural Standpoint*, St. Louis: Thomas Law Book
Co, 1948. Reprinted by Baker in 1982.

[68] **Ross Richard Clifford** (1951–) is a former Australian solicitor and barrister, and now Principal of Morling College, Sydney. Clifford's 1987 MA thesis at the Simon Greenleaf School of Law was *The Case of Eight Legal Apologists for the Defence of Scripture and the Christ Event*. The thesis was adapted for publication in Russian and English. Originally released as *Leading Lawyers Look at the Resurrection*, Sutherland: Albatross, 1991. Reprinted by Albatross in 1993 as *The Case for the Empty Tomb*. Missionswerk Friedensstimme in Gummersbach, Germany released the Russian version in 1991. An Arabic edition was published in 1997 by the Logos Center in Texas. The current English edition is *Leading Lawyers' Case for the Resurrection*, Edmonton: Canadian Institute for Law, Theology & Public Policy, 1996. Clifford surveys the work of Bennett, Greenleaf, Montgomery, Robert Anderson, Norman Anderson, Lord Hailsham and Luckhoo in a cumulative case for the gospels and resurrection of Christ. He also documents that pop apologist Frank Morison [Albert Henry Ross] was not a lawyer. Clifford's legal apologia has also been employed in two books co-written with Philip Johnson: *Riding the Rollercoaster: How The Risen Christ Empowers Life*, Sydney: Strand, 1998. *Jesus & The Gods of the New Age: Communicating Christ in Today's Spiritual Supermarket*, Oxford: Lion, 2001.

[69] **Frank William Hanft** (1870–1956) practised law in Minnesota and then became Professor of Law at the University of North Carolina. Hanft deals with scientific materialism in *You Can Believe: A Lawyer's Brief for Christianity*, Indianapolis & New York: Bobbs-Merrill, 1952.

[70] **Lee Strobel** (1952–) is a journalist and a pastor and the author of *The Case for Christ*, Grand Rapids: Zondervan, 1998.

[71]   **Earl L. Wingo**, *The Illegal Trial of Jesus: A Lawyer Reviews the Illegal Trial of Jesus*, Hattiesburg: n.p. 1954. Reprinted in 1962 by Bobbs-Merrill.

[72]   **Craig A. Parton** (1955–) practises law in Santa Barbara, California. His MA thesis at the Simon Greenleaf School of Law has been published as *Richard Whately: A Man for All Seasons*, Edmonton: Canadian Institute for Law, Theology & Public Policy, 1997. He is the author of two other books integrating law and apologetics. See *The Defense Never Rests: A Lawyer Among the Theologians* and *Religion on Trial: Cross-Examining Religious Truth Claims*. He is the United States Director of the International Academy of Apologetics which meets each July in Strasbourg, France and where John Warwick Montgomery is the International Director. See www.apologeticsacademy.eu

[73]   **James C. McRuer** (1890–1985) was Chief Justice of the High Court of Ontario and wrote *The Trial of Jesus: A Noted Trial Judge Analyzes the Events that Led to the Crucifixion*, Toronto: Clarke Irwin, 1964. Reprinted by Clarke Irwin in 1978.

[74]   **Albert L. Roper** (1879–1966) practised law in Virginia and wrote *Did Jesus Rise from the Dead? A Lawyer Looks at the Evidence*, Grand Rapids: Zondervan, 1965.

[75]   **Don J. Gutteridge Jr**, (1942–2021) is author of *The Defense Rests Its Case*, Nashville: Broadman, 1975.

[76]   **Kenneth Williams Linsley**, *Advocate for God: A Lawyer's Experience in Personal Evangelism*, Valley Forge: Judson, 1977.

[77]   **Roger Himes** is a lawyer in Denver and wrote *Counselor, State Your Case!* Denver: Accent, 1978. Himes primarily uses legal metaphor and analogies to illustrate matters of doctrine, but does include a brief section on the trial, death and resurrection of Christ.

[78]   **John Gilchrist** is a South African lawyer and Director of Jesus to the Muslims. Gilchrist co-wrote with

Josh McDowell, *The Islam Debate*, San Bernardino: Here's Life, 1983.

[79] **Jean Imbert** was Professor of Law at the University of Paris and wrote *Le procès de Jésus*, Paris: Presses Universitaries de France, 1980.

[80] **Charles W. Colson** (1931–2012) was a lawyer until the Watergate scandal. He employs a legal apologia in his book *Loving God*, Basingstoke: Marshalls, 1983.

[81] **Constance E. Cumbey** (1944–) is a Detroit lawyer who espouses a conspiratorial-eschatological interpretation of new age that most other apologists have rejected as untenable. Her twin works are *The Hidden Dangers of The Rainbow: The New Age Movement and Our Coming Age of Barbarism*, Shreveport: Huntington House, 1983. *A Planned Deception: The Staging of a New Age Messiah*, East Detroit: Pointe Publishers, 1985.

[82] **Wendell R. Bird** is a Yale law graduate and an apologist for the Institute for Creation Research. Bird has written *The Origin of Species Revisited*, 2 Vols. New York: Philosophical Library, 1987, 1989.

[83] **John Thomas Moen** was a Californian lawyer (d. 1996) who wrote an essay "A Lawyer's Logical and Syllogistic Look at the Facts of the Resurrection," *Simon Greenleaf Law Review*, Vol. 7 (1987–88) pp. 79–110.

[84] **David Samuel Prescott** was a Californian lawyer who wrote an essay "Antony Flew's Presumption of Atheism Revisited: A Christian Lawyer's Perspective," *Simon Greenleaf Law Review*, Vol. 7 (1987–88) pp. 137–162.

[85] **Herbert C. Casteel** served as a Missouri lawyer and then for 25 years as a judge. He wrote *Beyond a Reasonable Doubt*, Rev Ed. Joplin: College Press, 1992.

[86] **Dale M. Foreman** was a lawyer in Washington state and wrote *Crucify Him: A Lawyer Looks at the Trial of Jesus*, Grand Rapids: Zondervan, 1990.

[87] **Nicky Gumbel** was a barrister before he became an Anglican minister and the presenter of the Alpha programme. Some legal apologia is used in two texts: *Why Jesus*, Eastbourne: Kingsway, 1991. *Questions of Life*, Eastbourne: Kingsway, 1993.

[88] **John Grisham** is a former lawyer and the world's most popular novelist in the legal fiction genre. One of his novels is an apologia for Christian belief, *The Testament*, London & Sydney: Random House, 1999.

[89] **Gerard Chrispin** is an English lawyer who has written *The Resurrection: The Unopened Gift*, Surrey: Day One, 1999.

[90] **Ken R. Handley** is a retired Justice of the NSW Court of Appeal who has written the essay: "A lawyer looks at the resurrection," *Kategoria*, no. 15 (1999) pp. 11–21.

[91] **Paul K. Hoffman**, "A Jurisprudential Analysis of Hume's 'In Principle' Argument Against Miracles," *Christian Apologetics Journal* 2/1 1999.

[92] **Jeffrey C. Martin**, *A Lawyer Briefs the Big Questions*, Lexington: Bristol House, 2000.

Alphabetical Index
of Juridical Apologists

Scripture Index

NEW TESTAMENT

Index

JOHN WARWICK MONTGOMERY (Ph.D., Chicago, D.Théol., Strasbourg, LL.D., Cardiff, D.U.J. [*h.c.*], Institute for Religion and Law, Moscow) is Emeritus Professor of Law and Humanities, University of Bedfordshire, England; Professor-at-Large for 1517. (www.1517.org), California (U.S.A.); and Director, International Academy of Apologetics, Evangelism & Human Rights, Strasbourg, France (www.apologeticsacademy.eu). His legal specialty is the international and comparative law of human rights, and he is Honorary Chairman of the Academic Board of the World Evangelical Alliance's International Institute for Religious Freedom. He regularly pleads religious freedom cases before the European Court of Human Rights. He is a U.S., U.K., and French citizen, the author or editor of some sixty books in six languages.

Professor Montgomery is considered by many to be the foremost living apologist for biblical Christianity. A Renaissance scholar with a flair for controversy, he lives in France, England, and the United States. His international activities have brought him into personal contact with some of the most exciting events of our time: not only was he in China in June 1989, but he was also in Fiji during its 1987 bloodless revolution. He was involved in assisting East Germans to escape during the time of the Berlin Wall and was in Paris during the Days of May 1968. Dr. Montgomery holds eleven earned degrees, including a Master of Philosophy in Law from the University of Essex, England, a Ph.D. from the University of Chicago, and a Doctorate of the University in Protestant Theology from the University of Strasbourg, France, and the higher doctorate in law (LL.D.) from the University of Cardiff, Wales. He is an ordained Lutheran clergyman.

Dr. Montgomery is internationally regarded both as a theologian (his debates with the late Bishop James Pike, death-of-God advocate Thomas Altizer and situation-ethicist Joseph Fletcher are historic) and as a lawyer (barrister-at-law of the Middle Temple and Lincoln's Inn, England; member of the California, Virginia, Washington State, and District of Columbia Bars and the Bar of the Supreme Court of the United States; and *avocat honoraire*, Barreau de Paris, France). He obtained acquittals for the Athens 3 missionaries on charges of proselytism at the Greek Court of Appeals in 1986. He won the leading religious liberty cases of *Larissis v. Greece* and *Bessarabian Orthodox Church v. Moldova* before the European Court of Human Rights.

CRAIG PARTON is a trial lawyer and partner with Price, Postel & Parma LLP, the oldest law firm in the Western United States located in Santa Barbara, California, where he serves as Chairman of the Litigation Department. He is former Chairman of the Litigation Section of the Santa Barbara County Bar Association. Upon graduation from college, he spent seven years on staff with Campus Crusade for Christ (now Cru), the last four of which were spent as national lecturer for Crusade. Mr. Parton traveled to over 100 universities and colleges across the country, defending the Christian faith through lectures and debates. He received his Master's degree in Christian Apologetics at the Simon Greenleaf School of Law, an institution devoted to the integration of Christian faith and legal reasoning. Mr. Parton then took his Juris Doctorate at the University of California, Hastings Law School in San Francisco, where he served as Executive Editor of the Law Journal, COMM/ENT. Craig Parton is also the United States Director of the International Academy of Apologetics, Evangelism, and Human Rights in Strasbourg, France (www.apologeticsacademy.eu). The Academy meets for two weeks each summer in Strasbourg to provide advanced studies in apologetics to laymen and pastors. He is the author of "*The Defense Never Rests: A Lawyer Among the Theologians*" and "*Religion on Trial*." He has contributed to over 15 books and has published over 50 articles in legal, theological, and cultural journals.